BUILD YOUR OWN
OUTDOOR STRUCTURES
■ IN WOOD ■

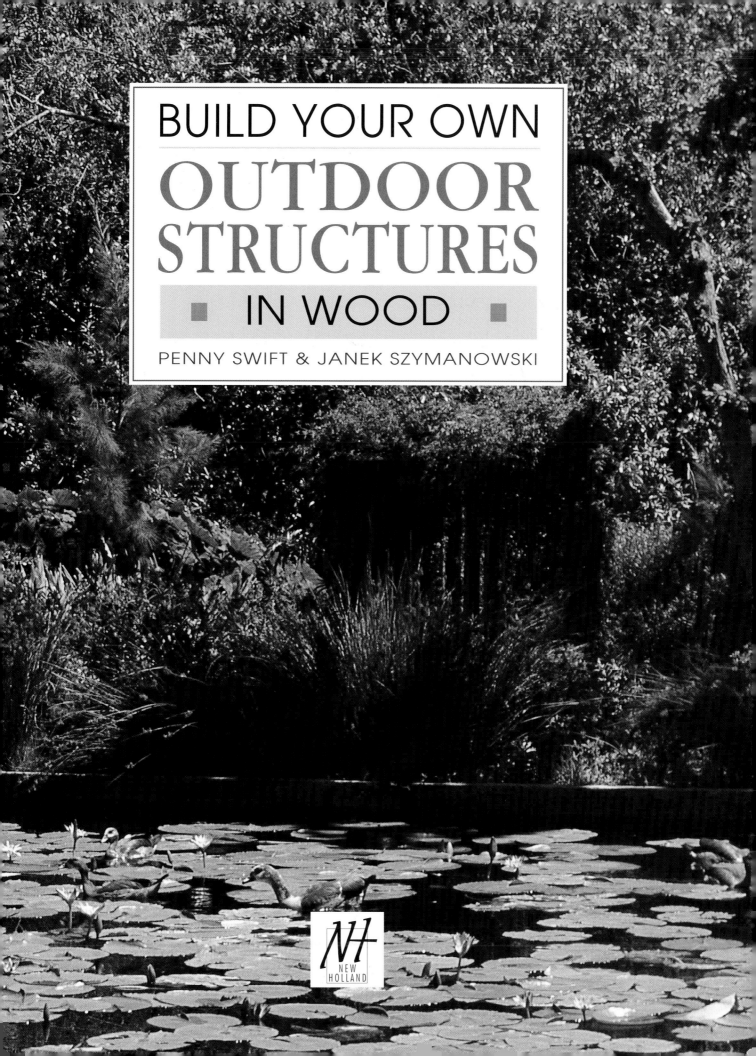

BUILD YOUR OWN
OUTDOOR STRUCTURES
■ IN WOOD ■

PENNY SWIFT & JANEK SZYMANOWSKI

NH
NEW
HOLLAND

ACKNOWLEDGEMENTS

A great many people contribute to making a book of this nature possible. These include professionals who assisted with ideas and expertise, ordinary home improvement enthusiasts who shared their achievements and difficulties, and all the wonderfully accommodating people with beautiful, interesting, or unusual wooden structures who allowed us to invade their privacy and photograph what they had built. Unfortunately we cannot list every person, but we want you all to know just how grateful we are.

This series relies to a large extent on practical information and step-by-step photographs as well as plans to inspire the reader. Three of the companies that helped make this book possible were Logo Homes, which builds lumber-frame houses and has a range available in kit form, Federated Timber Industries, and Mondi Timbers. More specifically, we thank Alan Cruickshank and Alan Paine of Logo Homes, Brian Reid, group product manager of Federated Timbers, and Dave Reeves, general manager of Mondi. In addition, a special thank you to Wayne Brown, a lumber-frame builder with extensive experience throughout the U.S., who graciously posed for pictures while building the step-by-step stud-frame structure featured on pp.46–50. Brian Buddle and John Marshall of Youngman Roofing, and John Mortimer, executive director of the South African Lumber Millers' Association (Salma) also deserve our thanks.

Those who checked the text prior to publication also deserve a very special thank you. They are Lewis Silberbauer, technical manager of Mondi Timbers, Steve Crosswell, regional director of the Portland Cement Institute, Western Cape, Richard Bailey, an engineer with the CSIR, and various experts based in Australia and the UK.

Many of the structures featured were built by ardent home handymen, others were professionally constructed. We do not always know which companies or individuals were responsible, and so we may have inadvertently omitted some names. In addition to the step-by-step stud-frame structure, the house on p.10 is by Logo Homes. Alan Cruikshank also helped Janek Szymanowski design the step-by-step pole structure on pp. 39–45, which Janek built single-handed. Four structures, designed by landscape architects Gouws, Uys, and White, are featured on pp.11,12,17, and 20. On p.12 there is a deck designed and built by Whirlpool Spa, and on p.16 a deck constructed by Mike Lister. Architect Margie Walsh designed the pergola on p. 55. Cerf's Adventure Playgrounds created the structure on pp. 56–57; and on p. 24 (left), there is a playhouse designed and built by Tony Mansfield, who also constructed the tree-house project detailed on pp.60–61. We are particularly grateful to Arne Schaffer of Cape Lumber who took the time to give us numerous locations. They include the cabin on pp.11,13, and 26, the bonsai shelter on pp. 9 and 22, the gazebo on p.14 (left), and the lumber umbrellas featured on p.29 and in the project on p. 54. The valuable input from all these people is gratefully acknowledged. In addition, a very special thank you to Linda Waterkeyn who completely redecorated the interior of her garden cabin featured on pp.13 and 26 (and also shown on p.11) especially for the photographs. A very special thank you to Pepe Sofianos and Don Watson, who designed and built the gazebo featured on the cover, as well as to Kent Reich of Disa Nursery for the loan of his pots and plants for the photograph.

Finally, we thank the publishing team, particularly editor Chérie Hawes and designers Julie Farquhar and Darren McLean, as well as Clarence Clarke for his meticulous illustrations in the plans section.

First published in the UK in 1996 by
New Holland (Publishers) Ltd
London • Cape Town • Sydney • Singapore

Reprinted 1997

24 Nutford Place, London W1H 6DQ, UK
PO Box 1144, Cape Town 8000, South Africa
3/2 Aquatic Drive, Frenchs Forest, NSW 2086, Australia

Distributed by Sterling Publishing Company, Inc
387 Park Avenue South, New York, NY 10016

Distributed in Canada by Sterling Publishing
C/o Canadian Manda Group, One Atlantic Avenue, Suite 105,
Toronto, Ontario, Canada M6K 3E7

Copyright © 1996 in text Penny Swift 1996
Copyright © 1996 in photographs Janek Szymanowski 1996
Copyright © 1996 New Holland (Publishers) Ltd 1996

Editorial team Chérie Hawes, Jenny Barrett,
Sally D. Rutherford and Hilda Hermann
Designers Julie Farquhar and Darren McLean
Cover design Odette Marais and Julie Farquhar

Design assistant Lellyn Creamer
Illustrator Clarence Clarke
DTP conversion Jacques le Roux
American adaptation American Pie, London

Reproduction by Unifoto (Pty) Ltd, Cape Town
Printed and bound by Tien Wah Press (Pte) Ltd, Singapore

ISBN 1 85368 665 4 (hb)
ISBN 1 85368 734 0 (pb)

CONTENTS

Wood is one of the most popular and versatile materials available for garden constructions. It is relatively light-weight, strong, and rigid, and has a pleasing appearance. Furthermore, with the most basic carpentry skills, it is possible to build shelters and simple buildings, decks, steps, fences, and a wealth of decorative features.

There are many reasons for choosing to use wood rather than other building materials, not least of which are the ease of construction and reasonable cost. It is usually quicker to erect a wooden structure and the process is less messy than working with bricks, blocks, or stone and mortar. Some wooden buildings are available in kit form, and small utility structures are often supplied prefabricated. There are countless design possibilities, ranging from traditional types to countrified units which blend well with the garden environment.

While the commonest wooden structures found in any garden are fences, walls, and steps, there are many more possibilities suitable for "do-it-yourself" construction, a large percentage of which can be built from wood, in all its forms.

Partial shade is created by a slatted roof.

The most obvious examples are pergolas (sometimes referred to as arbors) and walkways, many of which consist of a basic framework made from wood. Either attached to a house or freestanding, these structures may have a solid roof for shelter or be left partially open to the sky.

A deck is another popular type of lumber structure, with more complex variations featuring built-in seating, attractive handrails, and sometimes screen walls. Imaginative designs may also incorporate planters, spas and hot-tubs, and outdoor storage facilities.

Decking is particularly practical for sloping gardens or hillside locations, as it eliminates the need for traditional terracing which can be expensive and may not suit your lifestyle. It also overcomes the problem of cumbersome earthmoving and extensive landscaping.

Of course, wood may be used to build a conservatory or solarium, which will provide you with a welcome transition from house to garden. Similar extensions, using a large percentage of glass, are also popular for hot-tubs or whirlpools, which many people prefer to site under cover in the garden.

A "glasshouse" does not have to be attached to the house. If located beside a swimming pool or tennis court, it can become a haven for relaxation and casual entertaining. This particular method of construction may be used for a utilitarian but traditional greenhouse, designed to trap the sunlight and protect the plants inside.

A simpler alternative for plant enthusiasts is a straightforward, wooden lean-to where pot plants are sheltered and adequately shaded from sun, wind, hail, or snow. Even a freestanding structure can easily be constructed around a very basic framework of wood, using either fiberglass or an awning material such as shadecloth or canvas for protection.

If you are a bird-lover, a garden aviary or even a raised bird-house or covered bird-feeding table for wild garden birds may appeal. Dog kennels, too, may be constructed from wood, and if you live in the country, and keep poultry, it is the most obvious material to use for a simple A-frame shelter. You may want to tackle a more elaborate gazebo with latticework, or a traditional pavilion similar to the bandstands sometimes found in public parks.

For those who are lucky enough to live alongside a stretch of water, a lumber boathouse is a useful project. Another option is a dual-purpose shelter which can be used as a summerhouse as well as for storing movable garden furniture and other items not required indoors. Bridges, too, may be constructed from wood, whether designed for the practical purpose of crossing water, or purely as a decorative feature in a water-garden.

For families with children, a wooden play structure can be a most rewarding project. Tree-houses are an all-time favorite, but they must be securely fixed in the branches to prevent accidents. A simple platform built in a sturdy tree will provide hours of fun, and you can erect a small deck around the trunk so that the lumber floor doubles as a roof for a makeshift shelter below. It may be necessary to build a step-ladder for easy access.

The simple wooden structures described in this book cover most of the above options, as well as lumber extensions and additions. You will find various options for a range of utility buildings, including garden sheds and outdoor workrooms or studios, although we have avoided buildings larger than 556 sq. feet in size. There is also a section on building methods which will help you adapt the various projects to suit your own needs.

The focus of the book is on wooden

structures which are practical rather than simply decorative, but there is advice on improving the appearance of an existing structure or one that you plan to build. You will find that a coat of paint or the addition of latticework, wooden cut-outs, and fretwork, or potted and hanging plants, will give ordinary structures a special charm. Photographs throughout the book aim to inspire, while the accompanying text gives sound, practical advice and a host of good ideas.

The first section will help you to plan your project systematically and sensibly. It will enable you to identify your own needs and determine exactly what and where you should build. It will also help you to estimate the cost of the project and decide whether or not professionals should be employed.

Various design options are discussed and illustrated, ensuring that your structure will look attractive and will be compatible with the garden plan as a whole, whether it is a gazebo, a children's playhouse, or a practical toolshed. In addition, a wide range of flooring and roofing possibilities are considered.

For those wanting to build a traditional lumber structure, there is some interesting information relating to small pavilions, gazebos, arbors, and pergolas. The history of more substantial garden houses, country shacks, and other small, open shelters which were usually built of wood, is also examined.

Materials are discussed and the relevant tools detailed, along with various construction methods which are clearly explained (we have also included a section on plumbing and electrical work.)

There is a section of step-by-step photographs, showing you how to build a range of structures. Although it follows the construction of only two structures – a pole structure and a stud-frame structure – the instructions and illustrations also guide you through a simple method of deck-building, explaining how railings are built, decking slats installed, and how to assemble tongue-and-groove flooring.

The sliding doors of this "glasshouse" may be opened wide when the weather is right.

A simple, wooden bird-feeding table.

Reeds clad this delightful hide-out.

Two possible construction procedures for walls are described. One uses pre-assembled panels, and the other, the pole-building (or stick- frame) method. You can also see how windows and doors are fitted, and how a simple roof is erected.

The latter part of the book contains a series of ten different plans, together with detailed check-lists of materials.

Although formal building plans may be required for these designs (see page 10), they may be used as presented, or adapted and changed to suit your own needs and location.

Whether you aim to do all of the work yourself or plan to employ others to help, *Build Your Own Outdoor Structures* in Wood is an invaluable guide to have to hand at all times.

PLANNING AND PREPARATION

Careful planning is essential, even for the simplest of lumber structures. It pays to evaluate your needs carefully at the outset and establish exactly what purpose you want the structure to serve. Decide where you want to locate it and make sure there are no obstacles or major disadvantages in that position.

Unless you are fortunate enough to have an unlimited budget, costing the project in the planning phase is also imperative. Make the changes in the initial stages rather than wait until you have a half-built structure.

Even if you are determined to do-it-yourself, you may have obvious difficulties at this early stage, and it is often best to call in professional assistance (see pages 9–12) before you begin. You can always minimize costs by doing a lot of the hard, physical work yourself at a later stage.

YOUR NEEDS
Your own preferences and the needs of your family should help you to determine exactly what to build. Most of these considerations are practical and you can be guided by commonsense. Nevertheless, a little extra thought and preparation will ensure that you make the most of your building efforts.

For instance, if you are a keen gardener you may want a shed in which to store tools, a wheelbarrow, and potting mixture. So why not construct a shelter which will enable you to use it as a mini-greenhouse as well? Alternatively, a greenhouse may be built to house outdoor furniture. By locating it alongside your house or beside a pool, you can create the character of a traditional conservatory, with benches and pot plants, rather than just erecting a functional area in

which to pot and tend seedlings.

Even a simple deck can have many uses, and it pays to consider these from the start. By incorporating a pergola and wooden screen, it will immediately become more of an outdoor room, and by adding built-in benches and maybe a table, its function can be further extended.

A lot is dependent upon your lifestyle. If you want an area for entertaining, consider whether children will make use of it. You may have your heart set on a traditional gazebo, but if it is likely to double as a play area, it may not be a realistic choice. A larger summer-house, on the other hand, could be a far more practical option which would meet both needs.

Where space is at a premium, you may be able to create a multifunctional structure with an open area for seating and storage for tools and other garden items, such as pillows.

SITING THE STRUCTURE
Some wooden structures (including those which are assembled in factories) can be moved if necessary, but most are permanent additions designed to stay where they have been erected. Having established that you want a garden structure of some sort and planned its use, you must carefully consider where to site it.

You may be limited by space, but there will often be several possible locations in your garden. The best advice is to contemplate and explore them all, and to weigh up all the pros and cons before making a decision.

One of the most important factors is the accessibility of the structure, and this should relate to function.

You may want to use a deck for alfresco meals; if so, it should be close to the house (or, preferably, attached to it) and large enough to accommodate a table and chairs. If you aim to use it as a sunbathing

A clever solution for a hillside property with limited space.

deck, it should be adjacent to the pool (if there is one) or in a spot which remains sunny for most of the day. A garden shed is better sited out of view, but in a location which enables you to retrieve the lawnmower, wheelbarrow, and other large implements without difficulty or inconvenience.

A cottage or studio in the garden may be tucked away for privacy, but if you plan to work there and invite clients or customers to visit, it should be accessible from the road or from an area on the property where visitors' cars may be parked safely.

If you have lived in your house for some time, you will know which parts of the garden tend to be windy, cold, and damp, or uncomfortably hot in summer. If not, make a point of spending time outside and note the direction of prevailing winds, and areas which are constantly shaded from the sun. You may have found a site with a lovely view, but if it is too exposed, it may be unpleasant most of the time.

Wood is a sensible material for a difficult site, and obstacles like large rocks, trees, and even sloping ground

An attractive, oriental-style lattice structure designed to shelter bonsai.

can be turned to your advantage.

For instance, most wooden structures can be built on stilts (or posts) where the ground is not flat, and trees can be incorporated into your design. This will enable you to use areas of the garden which would otherwise be useless, but consider whether this approach will increase your costs.

EMPLOYING PROFESSIONALS

The size of your structure and the complexity of its design will influence any decision to seek professional help. Even if you are confident that you can do the building work yourself, you might prefer to ask an architect or designer to help with plans and specifications. If you have difficulty visualising a final effect, the solution may be to consult a landscaper or another specialist for ideas. You may know exactly what you want to build, but do not have the time or expertise to erect the structure yourself; in this case

Latticework and clever cut-outs transform a reasonably simple wooden structure.

Before you start erecting even the simplest wooden structure, it is always advisable to check on building codes and lot restrictions, as well as any possible legal restrictions, such as easements, which may be applicable. Find out whether plans must be submitted and if a building permit of any kind is required. Remember that you could find yourself demolishing or dismantling the results of many hours of hard labor if you do not have the necessary permission to build.

While some structures will not be regulated, it is universal practice to have specific rules which set minimum standards in the construction industry. You will find that many of these relate to safety (to ensure structures do not collapse and people are not injured), and common sense indicates that they should never be ignored. Even if formal plans do not have to be submitted to your local board or building department, it is sensible to

examine local regulations for guidelines relating to foundations and footings, lumber dimensions, the recommended height of structures, and so on, especially if you decide to build your structure without professional assistance.

In certain instances, structural lumber will be governed by regulations, and specified grades may have to be used. Where strong winds and snow, or even earthquakes, are a factor, it is particularly important to use adequately sized uprights (posts and poles.) The framework of any structure must be constructed in such a way that it can take the weight of the roofing materials if it is to be covered, and also with maximum wind speeds, snow loads, and seizmic forces. Various codes specify minimum spacings for wooden uprights and the depth to which they should be sunk into the ground, as well as the dimensions of foundations, footings, and other structural elements.

Suitable preservatives may also be stipulated (see page 29), particularly if a structure is to be used to house animals.

You may discover that there are limitations governing the location of wooden structures. You will need to work within building lines, and usually a specified minimum distance from the boundaries. In some developments, there may be a height restriction to protect the view of neighboring properties, and an architectural style may be specified.

Where formal plans are required, you will probably have to produce a site drawing, indicating the position of the structure, as well as elevations, sections, and drainage arrangements. If you are not using professional assistance, your local building department will provide a check-list of what is required. Note that plans based on the diagrams and illustrations on pages 52–63 will not usually be sufficient for submission to the authorities.

An A-frame garage made of wood.

A wooden cottage owner-built from a kit.

An attractive pergola, designed by a landscape architect, is sited over a walkway.

form part of a greater landscaping plan. Some professional landscapers prefer to subcontract structural work and concentrate on planting.

Contractor

The majority of small-scale builders will undertake garden projects and some will even suggest designs and submit plans. If you decide to employ a contractor to build your structure, ensure that he has the necessary experience and has completed similar projects. Ask for a portfolio of work completed to date or visit the sites of projects that he has already finished building. The best option may be to approach specialist contractors in your area, such as lumber merchants who sell prefabricated or kit-form wooden structures, and who may also build personalized, custom-designed units.

you may require the services of a building contractor.

Architect or designer

These trained professionals are well equipped to design garden structures which will blend with the existing architecture of your home. They should have a sound knowledge of construction materials and suppliers, as well as contractors and other experts. Most charge an hourly fee for consultations or agree on a specified amount to draw up plans and possibly even oversee the job. An architect (or landscape architect, see at right) will usually be registered or licensed with an official institute or body, while a designer may not have formal training or a qualification which is officially recognized.

Draftsman

If regulations call for formal plans, these should be drawn by a specialist. An architect or designer will certainly do this for you, but a draftsman will provide a less expensive service. In fact many architects and designers employ them to prepare their own working drawings. Although some draftsmen have good ideas and a knowledge of specifications and

materials, it is generally best to approach these professionals with a clear vision of what you want.

Landscaper

Landscape architects and garden specialists (who may or may not have formal qualifications), will sometimes undertake design and/or construction of garden structures, particularly if these

Subcontractor

A good compromise between doing all the work yourself and employing a contractor to do it for you is to enlist the services of subcontractors, providing that you have the time and energy to oversee the building work.

An experienced carpenter will be particularly valuable if the design incorporates complex joinery or

A lean-to alongside a lumber cabin is used for storing cordwood.

intricate decorative work. If there is glazing to be done, you may prefer to subcontract this part of the project. Glaziers will usually install the panes for an additional payment. Where electric wiring is required (in a shed, studio, or garden cottage, for instance), it is usually advisable to subcontract a qualified electrician, in fact your building department may insist on it (see page 13.)

Specialist consultants

Various consultants, including engineers, can provide valuable services, particularly if your site is an unusual or difficult one. If you are building on a steep or unstable slope, a structural engineer will be able to specify foundation dimensions, as well as wind- and load-stress calculations, and will advise on design.

A geotechnical or structural engineer will analyze the soil (if it appears to be problematic) and evaluate what steps should be taken to ensure that the structure is safe.

COSTING THE PROJECT

It is important to finalize your design in the planning stage (see pages 14–27) prior to quantifying and costing the materials required. This will help to ensure that you have the necessary funds and can budget carefully for each phase of the project.

First make a detailed list of all the materials you need, from cement, sand, and stone for foundations and footings, to nails and screws. Price the lumber carefully and try to avoid unnecessary waste. Standard dimensions and lengths are invariably cheaper than wood that has to be planed (or dressed) and cut especially for the job. If necessary, alter the design to suit what is readily available.

You will now need to cost labor. Find out what professionals, laborers, and subcontractors charge in your area. If any helpers are to be paid by the hour, always be generous with estimates.

Finishes and decorative features should also be included in the costing – even if you leave some of them until a later date (see pages 25–27).

An imaginative wooden arbor designed by a landscape architect for a park-like garden.

A hot-tub is set in an attractive deck constructed by a contractor.

Although all kinds of wooden garden structures are built without electricity or plumbing facilities, there are times when these conveniences make life much easier, or even when they are essential for the structure to be functional.

If you are planning on using your outdoor structure for entertaining guests or as a workroom, you may want running water, lighting, and a couple of power points for small appliances. Larger structures usually require more sophisticated facilities, but even a rudimentary tool shed will become a much more useful place with the addition of electrical sockets if you plan to use it as a workshop, and an outdoor cooking area will be more convenient if you have a plumbed-in sink, or at least a faucet. If you are ambitious, and plan to build a habitable structure, you may even want to incorporate a bathroom or kitchen.

You will usually need to hire professionals to undertake the work for you, but it is essential to plan for these services from the very start and to incorporate pipework, ducting, and so on, when you build.

Plumbing Building departments almost always insist that a registered plumber undertakes or at least oversees basic plumbing and the laying of drains in any building, and a wooden garden structure will be no exception. Building and health inspectors will be even more stringent if sewerage, rather than simply a water supply, is involved.

Piping and related materials required for plumbing should conform to local building regulations, but it may be

With imagination even a small structure can accommodate plumbing fixtures.

possible to use less expensive items than you would choose for your house. Using plastic (or PVC) rather than copper piping for the water supply, for instance, is a big economy.

Electricity Electricity supplied to homes by means of an underground or overhead cable is potentially dangerous, and should be handled only by qualified people. For safety reasons, the best advice to home improvers is to leave major electrical work to a licensed electrician.

If a pergola or enclosed patio is to be attached to the house, you will probably be able to utilize the existing wiring to provide additional lighting. Furthermore,

you may even be able to install new fittings yourself.

If you have built at some distance from the house, you may need a separate circuit altogether. Alternatively, the electrics could be linked to an existing outdoor circuit which, for instance, services a garage, swimming pool, or spa. Waterproof or armor cabling should be used underground where possible, and if light fittings are installed in an exposed position, sealed units must be used. If the regulations permit, you can lay cables and fix fittings yourself, but the wiring itself must be connected to the mains supply by a qualified electrician.

Wiring is fixed into the wall before paneling.

Hot-water pipes are fitted before the floor is screeded.

Whether you are building an elaborate gazebo, a garden shed, or a child's playhouse, it is essential to consider all aspects of design. Ensure that your structure is compatible with the rest of your garden design, so that it is an architectural and landscaping asset. There is little point in spending time, effort, and money on something that looks out of place or tacky.

existing trees and bushes you want to retain, rocks, and natural water. Indicate the direction of prevailing winds, as well as views which can be exploited, and note areas which get more than average sun or shade. To avoid any confusion and the need to redraw the site on paper several times, use an overlay of tracing paper for the new plan.

This does not mean you have to match materials exactly, or slavishly copy existing architectural styles. While these elements will be more important if the structure is attached to or is constantly visible from the house, a sensitive juxtaposition of contrasting materials will often add unusual character and interest, especially in the outdoor area or garden itself.

A simple gazebo provides shelter.

Another charming gazebo, made from poles and sawn lumber.

DESIGN BASICS

Successful garden design relies on a clearly defined plan which is carried out in an orderly fashion. If you are starting from scratch, decide on a basic layout for the whole area and determine where paths, walls, patios, service areas, and so on are to be located. Identify sections which will best accommodate a children's play area, kitchen- or herb-garden, pond or pool, and then decide where additional structures will go. Make sure from the start that all the elements you plan to introduce create a harmonious whole.

Whether you can visualize the final effect or not, it helps to work on a site plan drawn to a scale of at least 1:100. Draw in all existing buildings and features – the house, outbuildings,

Once you have a basic layout, you can decide which materials will be used for the structure itself and for hard landscaping (walls, paths, fences, and so on) and work on planting.

If yours is an established garden, the layout will already be determined and you will, in all likelihood, have a host of well-developed plants. There may even be existing structures and features which have been developed over the years.

Anything you decide to build in the garden must be part of the design as a whole, so it is essential that the style of a pergola, a gazebo, or even a simple shed fits the general plan. The structure should also blend with the architecture of the house and any existing outbuildings.

A lot can be learned from traditional structures (see page 17), many of which have been designed and placed to create a feeling of surprise and secrecy, for example, pathways that lead to sheltered arbors and shaded retreats, or plant-smothered pergolas and walkways that invite one to venture toward a rose- or herb-garden. Frequently, they are not seen in relation to the house at all, and so the suitability of materials is largely dependent upon the structure itself.

Gazebos, on the other hand, are generally built to capture a view and they are seldom tucked away out of sight. Although the range of whimsical gazebo styles recorded over the years relates directly to architectural preferences of the past, these often mirror the style of the dwelling. Thus, a steeply-pitched hexagonal roof could be tiled to match the roof of your house, or you could use inexpensive latticework without threatening the authenticity of the appearance.

Remember that pergolas and similar structures may be used to identify and divide the garden space. If they are also used as supports for colorful climbing plants, they will immediately add visual interest and welcome shade. Other structures, such as a gazebo or small pavilion, may be placed at a focal point in a formal garden, or designed as a feature of an outdoor entertaining area. A wooden bridge can enhance a water-garden, however small.

It is a little more difficult when designing a utilitarian building like a tool shed or animal shelter, but imaginative finishing touches can make all the difference. Consider painting a shed so that it blends with the surrounding environment, or mount a container below the window and plant it with colorful blooms (see pages 26 and 27.)

FLOOR SURFACES

In addition to esthetic considerations, the type of structure and its function will help you to determine the most suitable floor surface. While wood is often the obvious choice for a wooden structure, you may prefer to use a concrete slab, brick paving, or a ceramic tile surface instead. If the

USEFUL TERMS

Bargeboard Lengths of lumber, usually decorative, used to neaten the edge of the roof at the gable ends of a building.

Baseboard Wooden trim used to neaten the junction between internal walls and floors.

Batten Long, narrow, strip of wood, often square in section; commonly used as part of the roof structure, particularly when tiles, shakes, or slates are used.

Beading Narrow molding or strip used to neaten various elements in building.

Beam Squared lumber used horizontally at base of roof structure and supported at both ends.

Bearer Larger supporting beam or girder used at base of floor structure.

Capping Covering manufactured to protect apex of pitched roofs.

DPC Damp-proof course consisting of a membrane of waterproof material (usually polyethylene) laid under concrete floors and in walls to stop damp spreading through the fabric. A damp-proof membrane may also be laid under the roof structure.

Drywall The material used to cover and finish the lumber framework of the interior of a building. It consists of a board of pressed gypsum covered on both sides with heavy paper.

Fascia board Lumber used to neaten the back and front of buildings at the ends of the rafters. This is the surface to which gutters are usually attached.

Flashing Waterproofing which is used to seal the joins between the roof and various protrusions (chimneys, dormer windows, skylights, and so on).

Footing Term used for foundations, particularly of pillar, pier, commonly cast concrete, lumber post, or pole.

Foundation A solid concrete base (dug into the ground) on which a building or wall is anchored.

Fretwork Term given to various types of decorative trim fashioned from wood.

Gable The upper section of a wall at the side of a pitched roof, extending from the level of the eaves upward. Gable may also refer to a gable-topped wall.

Girder Large beam which supports floor joists. See also Bearer.

Half-brick wall A brick wall that is equal in thickness to half the length of a standard brick. A one-brick wall is built with two rows of bricks which are laid end to end, so that the thickness equals one brick-length.

Joist Parallel planks used to support flooring and decking slats.

Lath Thin, narrow strip of wood used for trellises and latticework. Also useful as a cover strip, for instance where sheets of siding or boarding meet.

Latticework Structure made with laths which crisscross diagonally or at right angles. Used as a decorative feature or for screening.

Plank Flat length of wood. May be used to form parts of a structure including beams, joists, and decking slats. Better known as 2x4 since it is generally 2 inches thick and four inches wide.

Post-and-beam A construction method using a basic framework of posts or poles and beams to support a structure, as opposed to *stud framing*.

Post A stout length of cylindrical or square lumber used as a vertical support in building.

Post anchor Metal plate or bracket set in or on a concrete foundation to anchor posts and poles.

Purlin Slightly larger version of a batten, usually used to support roof sheeting.

Quadrant Quarter-round lumber used to finish edges where two sides of a structure meet. Useful at external corners and in place of a coving at ceiling height.

Rafter Sloping beam that forms part of the framework of the roof. Lean-to rafters are found in mono-pitch roofs or over porches, stoops, and decks which are attached to a house.

Rail Horizontal lumber used in building. The term may be used in relation to various elements, such as drywall, a paneled door, or the top of a stoop railing.

Railing Arrangement of posts and rails (sometimes with diagonal crosspieces) constructed around the edge of decking, stairways, and so on.

Stay Prop or support, usually of lumber, used to brace a structure during the construction process.

Stick frame The framework of a structure put together using the post-and beam system.

Stud Vertical post of wood-frame houses and paneling or drywall.

Stud frame Framework for drywalling or partitions made with studs and rails. There are no vertical posts anchored into the ground, and the lowest rail, or floor plate, is nailed or screwed to the floor.

Trelliswork Crisscross structure made of wood or some other material, used to support plants or as a screen.

Truss Pre-manufactured or built on site, roof trusses consist of various rafters, beams, posts, and struts used to brace the roofing lumber.

structure is an extension of your house, you might like to continue the flooring used inside. When linking a pergola-covered patio, conservatory or additional room, this can be a very effective way of achieving visual unity.

In most instances, you will want a smooth, level surface, with a low-maintenance finish which is both durable and attractive. If the structure is open-sided, or partially enclosed but with no roof, drainage will be an added factor. Water must be channeled away from adjacent buildings and it may be necessary to slope the surface slightly (a gradient of about 1:40 is normal) to allow for run-off. The finished patio floor should be at least 6 inches below any damp-proof course (DPC) or vapor barrier in the wall of the building.

Any structure which is to be used for storage or play, for entertaining or even for work, however temporary, should always be built on a damp-proof base. A wood floor should be suspended above the ground and a polyethylene membrane laid beneath concrete and other hard surfaces. In addition to the more permanent hard materials considered here, you could use grass, stepping-stones combined with ground-cover plants, gravel, pebbles and so on to form an acceptable surface beneath an arbor or informal walkway.

Lumber

Lumber is relatively lightweight and easy to work with, and is appropriate for a wide range of structures including sheds, playhouses, workrooms, gazebos, and decks. The type of lumber used will depend on what is obtainable locally, but the basic choice is between softwoods and hardwoods (see page 28.) You will usually find that hardwoods are more expensive, but they are often better suited to exposed decking than a lot of the softwoods which are readily available.

Both square-edged and tongue-and-groove floorboards are suitable for garden structures. Decking slats may be slightly thicker than internal boards where a very soft wood is used, or where bearers and/or joists are widely spaced. It is best to choose lumber that has been planed (or dressed) all round in the factory.

Man-made board

Manufactured in various forms from lumber, most manmade boards are cheaper than solid wood.

Both ordinary plywood (made from several very thin layers of wood) and chipboard or particleboard (made from bonded fragments of wood) are suitable choices for the internal floors of sheds, playhouses, and similar buildings. Waterproof shutterboard (or shuttering plywood) is particularly strong and stable. All these materials should be laid over bituminous felt to prevent damage from rising damp and excessive moisture. Alternatively, the lower surfaces could be painted with a suitable rubberized bitumen sealant.

Unless particleboard has a veneer finish of some kind, it is usually best to paint it, or to cover it with polyvinyl sheeting. Plywood is reasonably attractive and can be left as it is.

A low-level wooden deck alongside a cabin in the garden is practical and attractive.

Split poles can be used as siding for garden outbuildings.

Wood has been used to build a wide range of structures and garden buildings for centuries. In Ancient Egypt, grape arbors were grown to provide shelter from the harsh desert sun, while in China, covered walkways and small pavilions were often constructed from wood. In Japan, wood was a primary material used to build traditional tea-houses, and in 19th-century England and Europe it was the obvious choice for rustic yet decorative utility buildings such as cow-sheds, chicken-runs, and barns.

For many centuries, bird-lovers have built garden aviaries from lumber. While early Chinese aviaries were usually crafted from bamboo, the Egyptians seem to have preferred wood. Nesting-boxes and bird-feeders, popular since the 19th century, have traditionally been made from wood. These small garden structures were generally rustic in style and designed to blend with nature.

The origin of boathouses can be traced to ancient China where lakes were a prominent feature in the royal gardens. Traditional Chinese bridges, which had decorative latticework along the sides, were often built from wood.

Galleries, pergolas, arbors, and open-sided walkways have been extremely popular in various forms for many centuries. Found all over the world, these range from colonnaded pergolas, so typical of both Ancient Rome and Renaissance Italy, to arched lath tunnels favored in 16th-century France, and the elaborate galleries preferred by the English at the same period. In colonial America, covered walkways were created in the gardens of the wealthy.

Decks, viewing platforms, and elaborate gazebos have had an equally long history. While the modern wooden deck is very often free-standing in a garden, or is used as a landscaping feature to terrace sloping ground, the traditional structure was more commonly attached to the house. Typical Japanese decks, for instance, led directly from the dwelling and served as a viewing platform to the garden beyond.

Some say that the gazebo, which is frequently constructed of wood, originated in the Netherlands, although the classic English gazebo is probably better known. Initially a feature of grand, formal gardens, it was invariably built in a location where there was a good view of the garden and the landscape beyond.

Unlike summerhouses, these structures were partially open-sided and usually square or octagonal in shape.

Although early pavilions were actually tented shelters, made of painted canvas and metal poles, by the 19th century many were being constructed of wood. Gazebo-like bandstands or music pavilions, which were mostly found in public parks and gardens, were also made of wood. So too were smaller sheltered seats, built in a range of exotic styles similar to those favored for a variety of garden buildings.

Small, open shelters, usually built of wood, were also popular in both China and early Japan. Roofing materials included thatch and bark shingles, and built-in seating was another common feature.

Although a greenhouse was the obvious shelter for growing seedlings and exotic plants in a cold climate, in some countries decorative lath or latticework houses were constructed to shade plants from the sun.

More substantial garden-houses go back a long way. In China, for instance, wooden shacks and structures with screened doors and windows were popular many centuries ago. While bnck and stone was more favored in some countries, in the United States, Australia, and New Zealand, garden houses and summerhouses were frequently made of wood. In the Deep South, for instance, antebellum summerhouses often combined solid roofs with lattice walls for shade and fresh air.

In England, where summerhouses were fashionable for centuries, they were originally called "shadow houses." While 18th-century versions usually mirrored the style and materials of the house, during the Victorian era, the style changed to rustic wooden buildings which were built by handymen and country carpenters.

Even tree-houses have a history. Since their recorded popularity during the 16th and 17th centuries, they have been called by many names including bowers, crow's nests (usually without a roof), and tree-rooms. Although generally thought of as play structures, pleached tree-houses (made by painstakingly clipping and training branches to form a room above ground), look-outs, or observation platforms built in tall trees, and similar structures were built in Persia three or four centuries ago, and were certainly not meant for children. Even the modern, well-built tree-house is sometimes used as a workroom or sanctuary for adults, or as a hide for birdwatchers.

An attractive gazebo with decorative detail, built in traditional style.

Concrete

Basic but versatile, concrete is frequently used both structurally (for foundations and footings) and as a smooth base for flooring. For instance, a stud-frame garden building, built from factory-manufactured panels, can be erected on a concrete slab (see pages 38 and 47-50.) The prepared surface is then screeded, and tiled, carpeted, or finished in any way desired.

Tiles

A wide range, including terracotta, terrazzo, slate, and clay quarry tiles, is well suited for use in the garden, both on patios and on floors within most outdoor shelters. These tiles should be laid on a solid concrete base, which is usually screeded to give a smooth surface prior to tiling.

Tiles which are exposed to the weather should always have a non-slip, matt finish, and if your area experiences frost and snow in winter, they should be resistant to freezing.

Bricks and blocks

Clay brick pavers, concrete blocks, and a range of simulated flagstones and pre-cast slabs are all possibilities for patio floors in a range of wooden structures. They can be used as

A colorful pitched pergola.

A fort made with poles and rustic timber incorporates a swing and an upper deck.

flooring for some gazebo designs, and even for workrooms and shelters used for casual entertaining. If the area does not have to be watertight and rising damp is not a factor, bricks, paving blocks, and slabs may be laid on a well-compacted base of sand. Otherwise it is best to throw a concrete slab (see page 38), if necessary over a layer of compressed hardcore, and to bed the chosen units in mortar.

SIDING

The majority of garden buildings made from wood require some form of external siding and, if you wish, internal finishing as well. Although metal has been a traditional material for cladding the exterior of some timber-frame buildings, it is not commonly used for ordinary garden structures. Instead, wood is a popular choice, and there are various options available, ranging from plywood sheeting to weatherboard and clapboard manufactured in different profiles. The choice of internal cladding is usually limited to either drywall or wooden paneling of some sort.

While most types can be affixed to the structure on site, some buildings (including sheds, playhouses, and even some quite substantial workrooms) are made from prefabricated panels. You may be able to buy ready-made panels, or you can make them by assembling the basic framework in your workshop and nailing the siding to it before the structure is erected (see pages 46–50).

Plywood

An exterior-grade or weatherproof marine ply (ripped or used in sheets) is suitable for many garden structures. Ordinary plywood or the more decorative clapboard, which has false joins to make it look like vertical or horizontal timber boarding, may be used to panel internal walls and partitions. The basic material is also useful for adding rigidity to prefabricated wall panels.If you wish, you can slice plywood into narrow widths and nail them in place so that they overlap one another slightly. This look similar to weatherboarding, as the overlap creates its own angle.

Rounded loglap siding on this shed creates a rustic, weather-resistant finish.

Shiplap (top) and natural wood siding

Hardboard
Available in sheets, this manmade board (made of compressed and processed wood-pulp fiber) is favored in some parts of the U.S. as a wall covering for sheds and barns. Seams may be hidden by nailing battens or cover strips of wood over them to create a more decorative effect.

Particleboard
Only exterior-grade particleboard is suitable for use as siding. When properly treated, it has a high resistance to water. It expands, however, so a suitable expansion joint filler must be used between boards.

Sawn lumber
Ordinary 2x4s may be used to clad a wood-frame structure, although it may be necessary to use battens or cover strip, either internally or externally, over the joins. This is a relatively labor-intensive option, but one which may be used when tongue- and-groove or other overlapping boards are not available. Alternatively, the planks may be affixed to plywood or another sort of paneling.

Trellises and lattice panels made from thin strips of sawn lumber may be used for screen walls or to enclose structures which are left partially open to the elements.

Weatherboard
A popular and attractive option, weatherboard is designed so that the horizontal boards overlap one another slightly. The profile you choose will affect the visual appearance of your structure. The most common types include traditional shiplap cladding board (see page 46), a rounded loglap, which gives the impression that the building has been made from logs, and slightly splayed lapboard.

Vertical boards
Both tongue-and-groove boards (if sufficiently thick) and V-jointed boards may be used vertically to clad garden buildings. As the widths and sizes of tongues and grooves may vary, it is best to buy all your lumber from one supplier. Some weatherboard may be affixed vertically, although this not generally recommended.

Fibercement
Made of a mixture of organic fibers and cement, high-density fibercement cladding is relatively heavy and so better suited to the larger garden structure. It can be pressed during manufacture to give the impression of woodgrain once it is painted.

PVC (polyvinylchloride)
PVC is another siding option which can be made to resemble wood. It is attached in the same way as wooden siding and can be used internally and externally.

Drywall
Drywall is only suitable only for internal use. The joints should be taped and then skimmed with a thin coat of gypsum plaster prior to painting.

Climbing plants cover a simple, painted structure.

A striped awning creates shade on a patio.

ROOFING OPTIONS

Even though somewooden structures are open-roofed, many provide at least partial shelter from the elements. Some arbors, pergolas, walkways, and many other overhead structures may simply shade or define the area, while summerhouses and a variety of pavilions and gazebos will give added cover from rain, wind, and snow. More substantial structures, including tool sheds, greenhouses, playhouses, cabins, barns, and log-cabins, usually offer full protection from the elements.

Plant ceilings

Creepers and climbing plants trained over pergolas, arches, and other garden structures will soon form a natural plant canopy which offers dappled shade. You may want to plant an evergreen climber, perhaps a jasmine or rambling rose, which will reward you with luxurious scent, or a species which bears colorful flowers. But choose your plants carefully.

A dense ceiling of creepers over a pergola constructed alongside a house will be a welcome retreat in summer, but may make the adjacent rooms gloomy and even cold in winter.

Here, it is safer to opt for deciduous plants which will lose their leaves in the fall. The many clematis species are great favorites, as is fragrant wisteria with its drooping racemes which precede thick, leafy cover in early summer. Bougainvillea is a frequent choice in warm climates, but although fairly hardy, it will not survive very cold, snowy winters.

Although creepers and climbing plants enhance the appearance of most structures (especially the more utilitarian types), you must ensure that the lumber is sturdy enough to support whatever you plant. Some mature plants can damage pergolas, arches, and so on with their weight, while others (including some types of ivy) may become invasive, pushing shoots through the siding.

Awning material

Used when shade is the primary requirement, awning fabric may not be waterproof and even the sturdiest fabrics will last more than a decade, while some have a lifespan of only about four years. Nevertheless, some fabrics are water-resistant and all will add color and interest to gazebos and patio roofs.

Various types of awning fabric are suitable, including treated canvas and shadecloth, a woven material popular with nurserymen for years. It may be fixed in place to form a permanent roof over the structure, or fitted so that it forms a retractable awning. Although there is nothing to stop you making a retractable device yourself, specialist suppliers in most areas will custom-make an awning to fit your structure.

Trelliswork

Latticework and thin laths of wood affixed as open slats may be used as an open ceiling for a pergola or walkway, or as an attractive cladding for a pitched gazebo roof. Lumber used for this purpose should be the best quality available, and should always be treated. Choose a reasonably rot- and termite-resistant type if possible (see pages 28–29). Once latticework and trellises start to deteriorate, they look tacky and should be repaired immediately.

You may be able to incorporate ready-made lattice panels, but be sure these are of a quality consistent with the rest of the structure.

Reed and bamboo

Both reeds and bamboo make effective patio roofs. Although usually attached directly to a pergola or the purlins of a patio structure, unattached panels may be suspended overhead. This process is simpler if you can buy the material in woven rolls and all you have to do is trim it to size. Unfortunately, rolls are not available everywhere. Alternatively, you can string or bind lengths together to create your own panels.

Used on their own, neither bamboo nor reeds will do more than shade an

A small, outdoor tool shed covered with practical, weather-resistant roofing felt.

area. They may be used as a ceiling in conjunction with roof sheeting of some sort . This is a particularly good idea for a cosy log cabin or to shelter a patio at the side of a house.

If you are fortunate enough to find a supply of growing bamboo or reeds, make sure they are green when put in place. If they dry out before installation, individual lengths generally become brittle and difficult to work with.

Roofing felt

Nailed to tongue-and-groove siding, plywood, or some other type of boarding, roofing felt is an acceptable option for sheds, garden workshops, and greenhouses, and one that is usually chosen for prefabricated versions of these structures.

Roofing felt is sold in rolls of various widths and is well suited for flat roofs, those which have a very slight pitch, or for mono-pitch roofs which slope in only one direction. It may also be used as a base for shingles or shakes.

A larger-than-usual shed, used as a sewing-room, has a roof covered with bituminous felt.

An open lattice roof gives partial shade to plants.

Polycarbonate sheeting over a structure attached to a house.

Alternative types of matting may be used in conjunction with boarding. Like roofing felt, the material must be coated with bitumen or some other waterproofing compound to make sure that the structure is watertight.

Remember to check your local building regulations for acceptability. For instance, you may find that two layers of ordinary roofing felt will be required to finish a roof.

Sheeting

Various materials are used to manufacture roof sheeting, some of which are better suited to simple wooden structures than others. Favorite types include corrugated iron, polycarbonate which may be transparent, opaque, or tinted, and either smooth or corrugated, and both translucent and colored fiberglass, although you will get a disturbing color cast from green and some other

shades. A tough, lightweight sheeting made from organic fibers saturated in bitumen is ideal for cabins, cottages, garages, and even playhouses and sheds (see page 44, steps 38–40.) Although aluminum sheeting and siding is popular for houses in coastal areas where rust can be a problem, it is an expensive option for the average garden structure. Fibercement, although relatively inexpensive, is not generally suitable because of its weight. It may, however, be used for cabins and larger sheds.

While corrugated sheeting is available in a range of profiles, the simple S-rib is probably the most suitable for the type of structures featured here. Most roof sheeting may be used for flat and ridged roofs (with a minimum pitch of 5° to 10° depending on the material), but it is essential to make certain that the basic roof structure is compatible

with whichever type you choose. Check specifications for the maximum spacing of roof trusses, for purlin and batten sizes, and the standard purlin or batten centers which indicate how far apart they should be spaced.

When laying any type of sheeting, it is important to overlap consecutive lengths to avoid rain and moisture penetration. Holes should generally be pre-drilled and proper roofing screws used to attach the sheeting.

If the roof is pitched, you will need capping along the ridge, and if it abuts the wall of a house, flashing will have to be incorporated to prevent rain from seeping through.

Glass

The traditional material for green-houses and conservatories, glass is relatively expensive and not usually the first choice of the home handyman because of its fragility. It can also make interiors excessively hot and humid, especially if the walls and the roofing are both made of glass. While tinted and coated glass will help reduce some of the effects of direct sunlight (including glare and heat), it is also important to know what thickness and glass type (wire-reinforced, laminated, and so on) to use. Building regulations usually offer some basic guidelines, but this is one time when professional assistance can be crucial.

Shingles and shakes

A common choice for period-style gazebos, shingles (and slightly thicker shakes) were originally made from wood and still are in some parts of the U.S.. They are also made from asphalt, which is easier to install and maintain, and from aluminum and fiberglass. If shingles and shakes are not easily obtainable in your area, a similar effect may be achieved with either flat slate or clay tiles (see below).

Rooftiles

A large number of traditional garden structures, including gazebos and summerhouses, are built with tiled roofs. If your house itself is tiled, this

A pole structure with a thatched roof offers sheltered seating.

may be an excellent choice, as it will enable you to match materials. The weight of most tiles is an important factor to be considered, and you will need a sturdy roof structure to support them. In addition, to reinforce the structure properly, battens or purlins will need to be spaced closer together than those holding roof sheeting. As more lumber will be required for this roofing method, your budget must be adjusted to reflect this cost.

A wide variety of tiles is available, although you will have to consider the pitch of the structure. Smooth, flat slate tiles depend on a minimum gradient of 15°, while most cement and clay tiles require a pitch of at least 26°, unless a suitable waterproof underlay is used. Ridging tiles will have to be used unless the roof is mono-pitched and slopes in only one direction.

Thatch

A popular choice for open-sided summerhouses and detached pool rooms in many hot countries, thatch is generally used in conjunction with wooden poles rather than sawn lumber. An African-style thatched umbrella may also be constructed atop a single pole. Various grasses and reeds are used for this type of roof covering, which should be installed by skilled craftsmen.

As thatch is a fairly expensive item, even in those areas where the grasses grow wild, acrylic thatch has become popular in recent years.

A traditional-style gazebo, its roof covered with shingle-like tiles.

Wood is probably the most popular material used for children's play structures. Most playhouses are made of wood, and climbing frames are frequently built with debarked and planed poles. Sawn lumber or poles may also be used for play-frames and elevated decks, which often incorporate swings and step-ladders. Play-forts with ramps and ropes are also easily constructed from lumber. Simple sandpits may be made with planks of wood, while exterior-grade plywood can be used to make basic shelters, or to clad tree-houses. Smooth, exterior-grade plywood is also a possibility for slides, especially if it is coated with a plastic laminate of some sort. A metal or fiberglass slide could also be attached to the wooden structure.

Of course, children will eventually outgrow most play structures. Properly planned and built on a reasonable scale, a playhouse may then be converted into a garden shed.

A well-built tree-house can be used as a den for older children and teenagers, or even as a secluded retreat for adults.

It is particularly important to ensure that the lumber used for play structures is smooth and well-sanded to avoid scrapes, splinters, and snagged clothes. It should be well varnished or painted with a nontoxic, lead-free coating of some kind. Paint can hide defects, like split lumber or broken knots, so use an alternative finish for climbing structures or little buildings and hide-outs erected above ground.

For safety's sake,, countersink screws round all hard edges and make certain no potentially dangerous nails are left even slightly protruding.Of course, all play structures must be properly braced and built so that they are stable. Children weigh less than adults, but when several little people climb onto a structure together, it will have to be sturdy enough to hold their combined weight which can be fairly substantial.

Where space permits, play structures should be located in a separate part of the garden. However, a structure which is intended for toddlers or for very young children should be near to the house where you can keep a watchful eye without necessarily having to abandon household tasks.

Surface materials should be chosen with safety in mind. Where possible, falls must be cushioned. Grass is a universal favorite, even though it does tend to deteriorate under structures and in constant traffic areas. Sand is another possibility, and it is essential to use clean, coarse sand. Some building sands may be suitable, but make certain that lime has not been added as it can be harmful to the skin. Avoid ordinary garden dirt as it will become muddy and stain clothes. Bark chips are very popular in some areas as they offer a safe and stain-free landing. Gravel is not a good idea as it tends to graze and can be messy.

A playhouse on stilts promises hours of fun.

A pretty little playhouse at the bottom of the garden.

INTERIOR FITTINGS AND FIXTURES

A variety of fixtures and fittings, including built-in seating, shelves, closets, sanitaryware, and various appliances, may be required inside your wooden structure.

A well-organized tool shed will need a workbench, as well as adequate storage facilities for handtools, machinery, and all those small items, like nails, screws, and washers, which are inclined to get lost easily.

A greenhouse will need shelves and working surfaces for potting and to accommodate seedlings and plants which are grown inside it, and a cabin used for sewing will benefit from shelving designed to store fabric and all the other items required.

There is no doubt that built-in storage is more practical than loose shelves and cupboards, especially when you are fitting out a small space. The type of structure you have built will determine the finish required, and in most cases, a handyman with basic carpentry skills will be able to do it himself. Quite basic arrangements are adequate for sheds and playhouses. For more complicated joinery, you may prefer to employ a carpenter.

Before installing closets, make certain that all the doors will open easily. In very small wooden structures it may be preferable to curtain the front of a closet or to install a sliding door to save space.

LIGHTING

Various aspects of lighting need to be considered, for both the inside and the outside of the structure. Decorative exterior lighting may be used to highlight foliage around it, or to illuminate the structure itself. More important is lighting which has a practical value. You need to be able to approach your structure safely at night and to illuminate the seating area if you are using it for entertaining. You will not need many lights, and even one fitting may be adequate. It is best to avoid harsh spotlights and to aim for a reasonably subtle effect. By placing several fittings strategically, you can accentuate plant forms and particular features, and add a soft glow to the surrounding garden.

Of course, an open structure may also be lit from within, creating a dramatic effect which is functional and decorative at the same time. For instance, a pendant lamp hung in the center of an old-fashioned gazebo will cast interesting shadows and introduce a welcome element of charm and warmth to the structure at night. Workrooms, sheds, and cabins may also be illuminated from within so that they can be used after dark.

Light fittings used in enclosed structures will be the same as any others used for the home. Those installed in the garden, on patios, or in structures which are even partially exposed to rain and moisture must be sealed units. These are available in a selection of styles and it is sensible to choose fittings which will complement whatever you have built.

Connecting the electrics calls for specialist knowledge (see page 13.) You will need to use suitable water-proof cabling or ducting, preferably buried underground, and to ensure the equipment is grounded.

FINISHES AND FINISHING TOUCHES

Having built your own wooden structure, it is important to finish it off properly and attractively. You will, of course, want a finish that protects the wood against weathering and decay, but appearance is equally important.

Steps combine a weatherproof finish with attractive fretwork.

A tiny cabin for guests, charmingly fitted and finished.

Plants and ornaments add charm to an ordinary garden shed.

prevent resin from seeping through the paint, and seal nail-heads to stop them rusting and discoloring paint.

To retain the grain of the wood but change the color, use a stain or a polyurethane wood coating. If you cannot find the color you want, stain the lumber before coating it. However, polyurethane varnishes tend to yellow and so change color.

Decorative detail

Various types of decorative work and trim may be added to wooden structures. Ornamental railings not only finish off a deck and make it safe, but they can also be extremely attractive. Latticework transforms an ordinary pergola into something quite special, while simple wooden cut-outs and more intricate fretwork will enhance the plainest building.

If a structure has a porch or adjacent deck which is covered, consider installing a decorative trim along the front just below roof height. Cut it out of wood or buy precast decorative cast-aluminum or wrought-iron edging and corner pieces. Another inexpensive idea is to cut a pattern in plywood and glue this to the fascia boards or even attach it directly to the ends of battens or purlins (see page 44). It takes little

For instance, a playhouse will be much more exciting if given a touch of color, perhaps just on the door and window-frames.A plain garden shed can become a charming structure if a decorative wooden cutout is attached to the fascias. If painted, it acquires a more countrified look and has a less utilitarian and austere air about it. Trelliswork,too, will add to the finish, especially if it supports climbing plants. Consider the area around the structure and decide where to plant or place containers and any other ornaments. You will find that these finishing touches make all the difference.

Finishes

Some finishes are intended primarily for the protection of materials, but it is important to consider their esthetic appeal as well. Unless structures are built in a period style or designed to match an existing building, and need to be painted, wood is often simply sealed for protection. This is usually the least expensive option and it may be the finish you desire, but it can look

bland and unimaginative. If you decide to paint the structure, always use a suitable wood primer to give it the added protection required outdoors. You should also seal resinous knots to

A rudimentary wooden shack, fitted and beautifully decorated for occasional guests.

The key to successful extensions and additions is to match materials and ensure that the old blends with the new. However, wood should be seriously considered even if the existing house is built with bricks and mortar. Although you may not save dramatically on materials, the erection of a lumber addition takes less time and requires less labour. Whether you employ others to do the work or intend doing it yourself, this will save you money.

If your house is plastered and painted, a an extension built of lumber siding may be painted the same color so that it blends in, and the roof structure can be duplicated exactly. Alternatively, wire mesh reinforcing fixed to siding allows for a variety of rendered finishes. The mesh must be about $3^3/_4$ inches away from the surface of the board to accommodate the sand-and-cement render, which should be about 5 inches thick. This coating is scratched while it is still wet to provide a key for the finishing coat, which may be as rough or as smooth as you wish. This construction method, developed in the United States, increases the versatility of a lumber-frame addition or extension.

For an existing facebrick house, the obvious solution is to clad the exterior walls with matching brickwork. The framework itself is lumber, and internal walls the same as those in any other wooden structure. Instead of using lumber cladding which is attached to the framework, a brick veneer is laid alongside or adjacent to the lumber stud frame. This usually consists of a half-brick wall which does not support the roof structure or any other load, but which is securely braced to the frame.

A wood-frame extension to a facebrick house provides work space for the owner.

Another common option is to use wood for a second story. Weatherboards complement both facebrick and a plastered or rendered finish, and many wood-frame homes are designed with brick cladding or even solid brick walls beneath and wood above. Rooms created in existing roof spaces are usually constructed with a lumber framework.

One of the simpler extensions to build is a glasshouse or conservatory attached to your house. To avoid leaks during wet weather, it is important that it is properly sealed, especially where the addition meets the existing building. Also ensure that it is well ventilated. While any conservatory should be light and bright,but it can become excessively hot on sunny days, and shades, awnings, and reflective film can help reduce the effect of the sun's glaring rays.

Although standardized modular conservatories are offered by various specialist companies, many of these structures are made with an aluminum framework rather than wood.

effort with a jigsaw, yet will elevate most wooden buildings from the mundane in an instant.

Plants

Planting invariably improves the appearance of any structure. Many structures are planned with climbing plants and creepers in mind (see page 20.) Flower beds should be considered as part of the garden plan as a whole, but also in relation to the structure. Plant on either side of the door leading into a cabin, or on three sides of a pergola. Introduce pathways leading to the structure and plant a herbaceous border on both sides.

Tubs, pots, and barrels will add character to a deck, while a window box will introduce color and enliven the front of a shed or playhouse. Hanging baskets are a charming addition to a pergola. Just be sure they are not in the direct line of prevailing winds or they could be damaged.

Ornaments

There is no need to be ostentatious, but some form of ornamentation can add an element of originality and individuality to a simple garden structure. A weathervane on top of a gazebo, a statue at the end of a patio, or a plaque or decorative panel mounted on the structure itself are all possibilities. Remember that any ornament chosen should be in keeping with the structure and the garden, in style as well as in scale.

The essential material for any wooden structure is, of course, lumber. The type chosen will depend largely upon what you are planning to build. While poles are suitable for pergolas and some rustic structures, most buildings will be constructed from sawn and often planed (dressed) hardwood or softwood. In addition to the lumber, you will probably need concrete for foundations as well as nails, screws, and bolts to fasten the various components. If there is glazing to be done, you will require glass. For roofing, you will need sheeting, tiles, slates, shakes, or thatch (see pages 20–23).

If you plan to work or even stay overnight in the wooden structure, internal paneling or drywall and insulation materials are essential. See pages 18–19 for a range of ideas.

LUMBER

The exact wood chosen for various garden projects will vary depending on what is available in your location as well as what is best for local weather conditions. In general, the choice is between softwoods and hardwoods, some of which are better suited to

A typical example of softwood siding.

particular structures than others. You will also need to decide whether you want to use poles or sawn (and sometimes planed or dressed) lumber.

Whatever your choice, it is essential to buy wood that is structurally sound and will be durable. Even if you are erecting the smallest shed or lean-to, it is good building practice to select lumber treated with preservatives for structural use. Also consider the intended function of the structure and the method of construction to be undertaken. Remember that the workability and nail-holding capacity of different woods vary.

Once you have bought the lumber for the project, store it under cover until you need it. It will deteriorate rapidly if left exposed outdoors or in damp conditions. If you have to leave it outside, stack it at least 12 inches above the ground with spacer blocks to aid the movement of air, and cover with plastic or a tarpaulin.

Softwood

Softwoods are cut from coniferous wood and are easier to saw and plane than most hardwoods. Trees felled commercially for construction in the U.S. include pine, red and white cedar, fir, , spruce, redwood, and hemlock. Since different species have different qualities, you will find that certain softwoods are more hardy than others. Redwood, for instance, is durable and renowned for its resistance to decay, while the wood from some fast-growing pines requires frequent maintenance if it is to last for any length of time.

Your choice should always be based on the best quality available at the most economical price.

Hardwood

Generally more costly than softwood, hardwood comes from various broad-leafed tree species. Some of the more usual types used in various parts of

the U.S. include mahogany, oak, species of eucalyptus, ash, elm, maple, and birch.

Although many people limit their use of hardwood in the garden to outdoor furniture, several species are particularly well suited to deck building.

Even though the classification 'hardwood' is a botanical one and does not refer to the durability, strength or "hard" qualities of the wood, hardwoods are often tough and very difficult to cut. This means that most need to be pre-drilled when nailing.

Poles

Poles are best-suited for pergolas and upright supports of decks and rustic shelters. They are also suitable for arches, bridges, and similar load-bearing structures. While this type of lumber may be combined with sawn wood (see below), its versatility should not be underestimated. For instance, if you need flat sections, you can use split poles or even boards cut in a loglap profile. Furthermore, they are suitable supports for thatch or even for some kinds of roof sheeting.

There is usually a choice between poles that have been debarked (and branches removed), and those that have been machined to a smooth surface and reasonably regular size. Poles that have not been machined will taper, quite obviously, from top to bottom, and two poles will never be identical. Even those that have been milled are slightly irregular in diameter. This characteristic adds a countrified appeal, but will not suit all structures.

Sawn lumber

Most lumber sold commercially for construction purposes is sawn in the mill to form planks, beams, battens, posts, and so on. Although rough-sawn lumber is widely available, many people prefer to buy it planed all round (PAR) or dressed all round (DAR); this makes it slightly more expensive, but gives it a smoother finish which makes it easier to work with. To finish a garden structure built with PAR (DAR) lumber, simply give it a light sanding and then oil, seal, or paint it.

A recently fashionable type of siding lumber has an uneven edge with some of the bark remaining. If it is available, it would look attractive as siding for a rustic shed, studio, or workroom.

The lengths and sections of all lumber components must be compatible with the scale of the structure itself. For instance, the garden shed featured on pages 52–53 uses $2^3/_4$ x $2^3/_4$ inch PAR (DAR) upright posts, but these will not be sturdy enough for much larger structures. Roof timbers must be chosen with the proposed covering in mind, as this will affect the design of the roof as well as the dimensions of purlins which support roof sheeting, and battens supporting tiles.

Standard sizes do vary, but this is seldom a major issue. In fact most suppliers will always quote nominal sizes, without taking the wastage lost during planing into account.

Lumber sizes are given as a guide in the plans featured on pages 52–63. If the exact dimensions are not available, you can have lumber planed to size, which can be expensive, or simply use the nearest size available and adapt accordingly.

If your structure requires long pieces of lumber you may have a problem, as world supplies of long lengths have become increasingly scarce. An international solution, based on a German invention, is finger-jointed wood, accepted worldwide as a strong and reliable method of lengthening structural lumbers in the factory. Alternatively, you can buy laminated lumber, which is more expensive but considerably stronger and more stable than wood sawn from a single log. It is also reasonably simple to join two lengths by bolting, screwing, nailing, or using wood connectors.

If the necessary thickness is not available, you can probably glue and clamp two lengths together. Just be sure to use a suitable waterproof

A wooden umbrella (see plan on page 54) on a waterfront deck.

woodworking adhesive which will resist temperature changes and moisture.

Quality

Lumber, both native and imported, is graded throughout the U.S. There are certain important points to remember about grades. .

For instance, all newly felled "green" lumber contains a large percentage of water and the wood must be dried to strengthen it. In factories, this is done either in huge kilns or by air-seasoning, where the wood is allowed to dry out naturally. Both processes kill the spores of fungi and destroy pests including termites and beetles, as well as their larvae and eggs. Be guided by the grading. Poor grades of wood may still contain a high degree of moisture.

Avoid twisted, bowed, or split lengths of wood as these defects can affect the stability of any structure. Sawn wood with an excessively sloping grain should also be avoided as it is more likely to warp, while too many knots, especially hard, dead knots from old branches, are undesirable as they are liable to fall out and cause weakness.

Preservatives

Some wood, such as heart-grade redwood, is naturally resistant to fungal decay and infestation, but the best advice to amateur builders is to use lumber which has been pressure-treated in the mill. If you do not treat wood adequately it will rot, and insects,

termites, and other parasites will eventually destroy it. On the other hand, if it is treated according to recognized specifications, it will be as durable as most other materials.

There are three basic types of preservative, coal tar creosote being the cheapest and probably the best known to home improvers. Although creosote is suitable for outdoor use and useful for coating the ends of poles and posts in the ground, it is highly toxic to plants and will cause some materials, such as shadecloth (see page 20), to rot. In addition, it has a strong smell and cannot successfully be coated with paint or any other finish.

Certain types of organic solvent-based preservatives, including PCP (pentachlorophenol) and TBTO (tributyl tin oxide), are also toxic.

Water-based preservatives are usually colorless and odorless, and can be easily coated with a finish. However some of these products, such as CCA (chromated copper arsenate), which is commonly used for pressure-treating poles and roof timbers, give the wood a slightly green tinge. Although CCA can be used outdoors, many of the water-based preservatives (including boron) are suitable only for interior wood. Toxicity levels vary, but treated wood should never be burnt in an open fire or used for a barbecue (see page 37).

CONCRETE, MORTAR, AND PLASTER

Concrete and mortar, as well as various plasters (renders), and floor coatings, are necessary for foundations, footings, and any solid slab floor.

Mortar is used for bricklaying, rendering external walls, and screeding concrete floors. Any building that has internal drywalling may be skimmed with gypsum plaster or with special skimming plaster.

The common components of concrete and mortar are cement and sand. Stone is added to concrete to add strength and give bulk to the mixture. Lime mixed into mortar will improve its plasticity and cohesiveness and aid water retention. This helps avoid cracking once it hardens.

Cement

Although there are various types of cement, Portland cement is most commonly used. Packaged in 100 pound or 80 pound sealed paper sacks, it hardens when mixed with water and gains its strength by curing, which involves keeping it damp for a period of time. While it is in storage, cement must be kept absolutely dry. Never leave bags outside, and stack them above floor level.

Aggregate

Various aggregates are mixed with cement to form concrete and mortar. Generally, material that can pass

Screeding a floor with mortar.

through a 2-inch sieve, like sand, is referred to as fine aggregate, and coarser material (usually crushed stone) as coarse aggregate. Mortar contains only fine aggregate, while concrete includes both forms.

Suppliers of coarse aggregate usually supply what they refer to as single-sized stone. Crushed stone is sieved and natural pebbles screened to size. Gradings may differ slightly, but the most common size used by amateur builders is $^{1}/_{2}$ or $^{3}/_{4}$ inch, and all quantities given in the plans on pages 52–63 refer to this size. Although it is less expensive to buy stone in bulk, it is also available loosely bagged from most builders' supply stores.

Sand, available from the same sources as stone, is also graded and should contain particles of various sizes. It must be clean and should not contain any clay or vegetable matter. You need fairly coarse or "sharp" sand for concrete, and softer sand for mixing mortar (used for render and screeds.) Bedding sand beneath paving bricks should also be coarse, while that used between the joints should be fine.

Most natural sand is suitable for concrete and mortar. River sand is usually quite clean and free of clay, while pit sand, although well-graded, may contain too much clay. Beach sand can only be used if it is thoroughly washed and processed.

Water

Water is a vital ingredient in concrete and mortar, and is not usually measured. Just enough is added to the dry materials to make them workable. It is vital to use clean, pure water. Seawater may be used for unreinforced concrete (it will cause reinforcing to rust), but the salt will leave a white, powdery deposit on the surface. A good rule of thumb is that if you can drink the water, you can use it for building.

Lime

Hydrated builders' lime, sold in 50-pound bags, improves the cohesiveness and plasticity of mortar, especially when coarse sand is used in the mixture. Otherwise, use a brand-name plasticizer.

Agricultural lime, road lime, and quicklime (calcium oxide) are not suitable for this purpose.

Concrete

The properties of concrete depend on the proportions of cement, sand, crushed stone, and water in the mixture. The proportions used depend on local conditions and the type of work you are doing, though low-strength concrete is usually adequate for the kind of construction described here. For foundation footings and solid slabs, combine the dry materials in a 1:4:4 cement: sand: stone ratio and add enough water to produce a workable mix (use a higher proportion of cement if you are building a large structure, or if the concrete is to be exposed to the elements). You will need about 500 pounds of cement for every cubic yard of concrete (or more if you are making a stronger mix).

Dry mixed materials are available for minor concrete projects, but these are relatively expensive. For larger projects, ready-mixed concrete is often a viable proposition. You will have to order a substantial quantity, and it must be used as soon as it arrives.

Mortar mixes

Mortar is the conventional name given to various cement, sand, and water mixes, and is used for bricklaying, rendering, and floor coatings or screeds. Hydrated lime is often added to the mix to make it more pliable.

As with concrete, the proportions of dry materials vary when you mix mortar. You can rely on a cement: sand mix of 1:4 for any bricklaying or rendering required here. Concrete slabs may also be screeded with a 1:4 mix. If you are adding lime to the mortar, combine it in the ratio 2:1:8 (cement: lime: sand).

Plasters

Exterior render (see above) is sometimes referred to as plaster, although the term refers more correctly to gypsum plasters for indoor use only. Plaster is mixed with water and applied with a trowel on bare brick, cement render, or drywall. There are various types, including special finishing or skimming plaster which is also available ready mixed in buckets. Although gypsum and skimming plasters can be messy to apply, they dry rapidly and create a really good, smooth finish.

INSULATION

Insulation can make the most basic structure habitable. It can also increase the potential uses a garden building can have. There are various insulation materials available, including fiberglass blankets, aluminum foil, treated vermiculite granules, and loose fill sold in fiber form. Most may be placed in the ceiling space or fixed into drywall paneling. Fiberglass and foil are best suited for garden structures.

Fiberglass

Blankets of fiberglass are useful for both ceiling and wall insulation. Just trim the sheets to size with a utility knife or panel saw, then lay them in the ceiling space, or position them in the walls before the internal paneling is secured (see page 49.) Fiberglass is easy to work with, but it can cause skin irritation so you must wear gloves and a mask when working with it.

Aluminum foil

Reinforced aluminum foil is manufactured in several grades, sometimes with a plastic vapor barrier on one side. It can be attached directly to both wall and ceiling panels prior to installation. If it is to be positioned once the roof trusses are in place, it should be attached between the rafters and the purlins or battens, with the waterproofing membrane uppermost.

FASTENERS

A wide range of fasteners and connectors is available for use when building wooden structures. Nails are the most common, but screws, bolts, and various special connectors are also useful. In addition, you may need reinforcing rods, hoop-iron strapping, and pieces of angle iron. Wherever possible, use rust-proof fasteners made

Aluminum foil is an effective material for insulating roofs.

from galvanized and anodized metal, brass, stainless steel, or aluminum.

Nails

Generally sold by weight and length, nails make a quick, strong and permanent joint provided the correct type is used. Various shapes and sizes are designed for different types and thicknesses of material. Oval wire nails have an unobtrusive head, making them suitable for the attachment of floorboards, and round wire nails are intended for fairly rough carpentry. Masonry nails fix lumber to concrete or brickwork, and ring-shank or twisted-shank nails will secure roof sheeting.

When joining two pieces of wood of roughly the same thickness, make sure the nail goes at least half-way through the second piece. If one section is much thinner, use a nail that is 2½ to 3 times the thickness of this piece.

Screws

Screws come in a variety of sizes and gauges. They are generally sold by number and diameter. Head shapes may be raised, rounded, or countersunk, and the slot is either straight or crossed in one of three patterns – Phillips, Supadriv, or Pozidriv. Gauges range from no. 4 (about the smallest you will need) to no. 12. Each gauge is available in a range of lengths.

Apart from ordinary wood-screws and chipboard screws (which have

a deeper thread and do not taper as much), there are special-purpose screws. Coach screws are useful when erecting wooden structures. They have either a square or a hexagonal head. Sold by diameter rather than gauge number, they are tightened with a spanner instead of a screwdriver.

Bolts

Bolts, in a variety of sizes, are the usual choice for heavy-duty fixing. Coach (or cuphead) bolts have a rounded head and a short thread, while hexagonal bolts often have a thread which extends the full length of the shaft. Nuts and bolts are tightened with spanners. Anchor bolts should be used for bolting lumber to bricks or concrete, as they expand in masonry to anchor the wood securely.

Staples

Heavy-duty staples are used with a staple gun for attaching awning fabric to pergolas or plywood to panels. They are "shot" into place and hammered lightly until the staple is flush.

Special connectors

The range of metal connectors and fastening plates includes joist hangers, post anchors, pole and truss hangers, various angle brackets, and spiked nail plates. They are made of galvanized or rust-proof metal and most are pre-drilled for easy use.

TOOLS AND TECHNIQUES

You do not have to be a skilled carpenter to erect most simple wooden structures. Nevertheless, your task will be simplified if you use the correct tools. You should also master certain basic construction techniques which will help you to build something that looks professional, and that will last.

TOOLS

An extensive toolkit is not necessary for most projects, but there are certain tools which are essential. If you need to buy tools, choose the best you can afford. If you are unlikely to use expensive equipment again, it is more sensible to rent rather than buy.

Setting out and levelling

All structures must be correctly set out before building work commences. Unless you are building an octagonal or hexagonal gazebo, you will need to ensure that all corners are square. The site or upper surface of foundations must be flat and level.

The most important tool you will need is a good quality retractable steel tape,

preferably with a locking mechanism. You will also need a metal builder's square and a spirit level with horizontal and vertical indicators. Choose a level that is at least 48 inches long.

One of the least expensive and most useful tools is a water level, made from a length of transparent tubing. It works on the principle that water finds its own level and is an invaluable aid when setting out on a slope, establishing drainage levels, or working out the correct height of poles and posts (see page 42.) A torpedo level is useful for leveling foundation sills and shelving.

You will need a pick if you are excavating hard or stony ground and a spade to dig foundations. Chalk (or even flour) may be used to mark the outline for footings, but it is better to use pegs and line to lay out the site accurately. Although you can buy pegs, any offcuts of 2x4 may be used and ordinary string may be substituted for builder's line.

Where compaction of the ground is necessary, use a punner or tamper. This tool, made from a wooden pole or

broom handle set in a lump of concrete is usually quite adequate. If the area to be flattened is fairly large, or if it is necessary to bring fill on to the site to level the ground, you may prefer to hire a compacting machine.

An auger is useful for boring holes if you are using the post-and-beam method of constructing a building (see page 40). It can also be used for sinking posts into the ground for a pergola, or for creating tube forms to contain concrete footings for decking post anchors. There are both manual and power-driven augers. If concrete is to be poured around the posts once they are in place, excavate holes that are wide enough to accommodate it.

Concrete and brickwork

Some of the tools used for setting out, including spirit levels and squares, are also indispensable for laying both concrete and bricks. Additional basic requirements include a builder's wheelbarrow and shovel for shifting dry materials, and mixing concrete and mortar, and straightedges for leveling concrete and checking brick courses.

Of course, you will need trowels for bricklaying, plastering, and possibly flattening concrete. A wooden float is essential for screeding a floor.

A brick hammer with a chisel end is useful for cutting bricks but an angle grinder is easier to use. Another tool used by bricklayers is the corner block, often home-made, which helps ensure that brick courses are level and even. Cut two L-shaped blocks from wood, saw a slot-and-groove through each, and wrap builder's string around them. They can then be hooked on to either end of a brick wall at the same height, and held in place with builder's line to establish correct levels. However, as foundation walls are usually the only brickwork required for a wooden structure, these blocks are not essential.

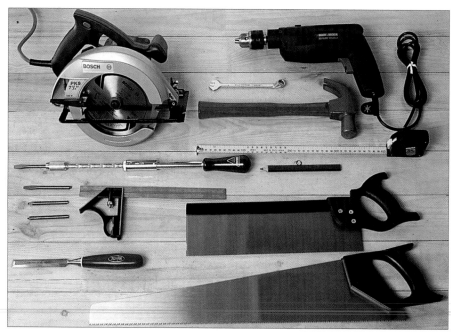

A basic toolkit, including both hand and power tools.

A belt sander will save you hours of hard labor.

A circular saw will cut quickly, smoothly, and in a straight line.

A concrete mixer is worth renting if there is a lot of concrete to be placed, as hand-mixing can be hard work. Concrete mixers are referred to by their capacity. A 10/7, for instance, can process 10 cu. feet of dry materials in a reasonable period of time, to produce 7 cu. feet of concrete.

Woodwork

Both hand and power tools are required in the carpenter's toolkit. You may be able to get by with the bare minimum, but there is no doubt that the better equipped you are, the easier it will be, and the result will be a more professional-looking structure.

First and foremost, you will need suitable cutting tools, including saws, although you certainly do not need every type available. Although you can get by without the electric models, both power jigsaws and power circular saws make light work of many jobs, cutting more quickly and smoothly than handsaws. While a circular saw will cut in a straight line at any angle, a jigsaw may be used to make curved cuts, and is useful for creating interesting cut-out patterns, bargeboards, and fascias (see page 45.) On the other hand, it is easier to be more accurate with a handsaw. For fine work, a robust

cabinet (back) saw is invaluable, while a crosscut saw or smaller panel saw is the answer for slicing the ends of posts, battens, floorboards and so on. If you are going to be working with logs or poles, it is probably worth investing in a bowsaw. You may also want a ripsaw, designed for cutting along the grain of wood, and a general-purpose hacksaw, which will cut any metal you may need.

Planes, rasps, and files are useful for shaping and finishing, while chisels are invaluable for trimming wood and for cutting notches and housings. While an electric planer is ideal for smoothing and sizing lumber, and beveling or angling edges, you are unlikely to need one, especially for the projects in this book. If you have access to an electric router, you could use it for cutting grooves and rebates, or for creating attractive chamfered edges on railings and so on, but this is not an essential tool for these projects.

While you will make use of an ordinary tape to measure wood, and a standard spirit level to ensure that it stands perfectly plumb, or is flat and level, a small tri-square or carpenter's combination square (incorporating a spirit-level vial) is a very useful tool to have. A chalk line is ideal for marking

the straight cutting lines on wood, especially when building with decking-slats and floorboards.

You will need a claw hammer for driving nails and extracting bent or incorrectly angled nails, screwdrivers for ordinary wood-screws, and spanners to tighten bolts and coach screws. Unless you plan to nail the entire structure together, you would be advised to invest in a good quality drill. A heavy-duty bit-brace or hand-drill will suffice, but an electric drill, even a small battery-powered model, is an invaluable tool to have. Do not forget to have a variety of appropriate wood drill-bits on hand.

Another useful tool to consider buying is an electric sander. A belt sander may be used to level planks and boards which have been smoothly planed (or dressed.) The smaller orbital sander is ideal for finishing a variety of small surfaces which might otherwise have to be sanded by hand.

Finally, you will need to have a flat and secure working surface. If you do not have a workbench in your tool shed, a portable workbench with built-in clamps is the answer. These usually fold flat, and may be packed out of the way when not in use.

SETTING OUT

Whatever you are going to build and whichever method of construction you use, it is essential to spend time laying out the site correctly.

Unless the structure is to be circular or have acute or obtuse angles, it is vital to ensure that all corners are square. This is a fundamental building principle which will help you achieve a professional finish.

Use pegs and builder's line or string to mark the perimeter, using a steel square to create a 90° angle at each corner. Alternatively, you can use a larger home-made square, using what is known as the 3:4:5 method. For this, three pieces of wood are hammered together to form a right-angled triangle. The two outside lengths should measure units of three and four respectively (say 36 and 48 inches), while the side which cuts the corners should measure a proportional unit of five (in this case, 60 inches). If the structure is sufficiently large, it is best to measure 9 feet, 12 feet and 15 feet respectively. You can also check the

accuracy of your angle with this method, using the steel square and a tape, or by staking the required measurements along the string line and then measuring across the angle. Once you have done this, double-check for square, measuring the layout diagonally from opposite corners. If correct, the diagonal measurements should be exactly the same. Once the basic layout has been established, mark the position of any foundation footings, using chalk or flour.

Levels

One advantage of post-and-beam buildings is their versatility on sloping ground. These may be structures built on a post framework or decking, taking the form of a pole platform without sides or superstructure. You need to establish the ideal level for the floor and the best position for all the upright supports, avoiding rocky ground.

If you are working on a difficult site, you may require the services of an engineer, but for a gradual slope it is not difficult to determine these positions.

Although many professionals use a torpedo level or a transit-theodolite, the surveyor's usual tool, the simplest way to establish these points is by using a water level (see page 32.)

Decide where the upright posts are to be positioned, and where the highest point of the floor structure will be (allowing for joists and bearers), then mark where bearers (or girders) should be secured by using a water level. This is done in the same way as illustrated on page 42, using the highest point as the reference level.

FOUNDATIONS AND CONCRETEWORK

Irrespective of the type of floor you choose for your structure, poles or wall panels must be securely anchored to a solid foundation. This may be a solid slab (see page 38), or footings. Either way, the depth and dimensions of the foundation must be designed so that the building can withstand all possible loads – heavy materials, wind uplift, rain, hail, and snow, and even mild seismic shocks.

Setting out a structure using the 3:4:5 method.

Upright poles are set in footings and braced in position.

The stilts of this A-frame play structure are securely anchored in concrete.

Concretework

The quantities of dry materials recommended for this type of concretework are given on page 30. Use a builder's bucket or clean 25-quart drum to measure accurately, do not rely on guesswork.

You can mix the materials with either a spade or a concrete-mixer. It is hard work by spade, but unless you have a reasonably large volume to mix, it is not worth hiring a mixer.

To mix by spade, you will need a clean, level surface or a builder's wheelbarrow. Combine the cement and sand first, making a hollow in the center for the water. Pour in a little at a time, shoveling the materials from the outside to the center, until they are well mixed and have a soft, creamy consistency. Add the stone last, with just a little more water if necessary.

When using a mixer, it is advisable to load the stone first, together with a little water. This prevents the cement from building up around the blades. Add the cement next, and then the sand and enough water to obtain a workable consistency. It should not take more than about two minutes.

The concrete mixture must not be allowed to dry out before it is poured. Since dry soil will absorb the moisture from wet concrete, it is essential to dampen the base of the hole before placing the mixture.

It is a simple matter to place concrete in footings. Use the back of your spade or shovel to push it firmly into the holes to level the upper surface. The trickiest part is ensuring that the posts remain absolutely vertical.

If you are throwing a slab, you will need a straightedge (2x4) to compact the concrete, using a chopping action to expel the air. At the same time, level the slab with a smooth, sawing action. Allow the concrete to set, ideally keeping it moist for five to seven days. This will aid curing and result in a really strong, solid base for the wooden structure.

It is usually necessary to screed the surface of a concrete floor to give it a smooth finish. This process is illustrated step-by-step on page 49.

Footings

If poles or posts are set directly into the ground, the hole (and consequently the length of lumber underground) must be considerably deeper than if it is encased in concrete. Furthermore, it is essential to compact the soil at the bottom of the hole to minimize settling.

Although decks are often built on pier footings, with upright posts anchored on to the upper surface of the concrete, this is not recommended for larger structures. This type of footing should be at least 8 inches deep. A tube form, made from cardboard, will enable you to leave a portion of the footing protruding above ground.

Suggested foundation sizes are given in all the plans on pages 52–63, but these assume you are building on flat and stable ground, in a location where abnormal weather and seismic conditions are unusual.

If frost, snow, strong winds, and earthquakes are a factor, all footings must be dug deeper. Numerous tables are available giving figures for greater loads. Alternatively, consult an expert or professional engineer for advice.

Where a structure is built on sloping land, it may be necessary to embed posts and poles deeper into the ground on the uphill slope for extra strength. The tops of all posts, apart from those at the apex of a roof, will be at the same level, but more lumber will be visible at the lowest points under the floor level.

Foundation slabs

If you plan to cast a slab on solid, stable ground, all you need do is compact the area thoroughly with a punner prior to pouring the concrete. If the ground is not firm and level, you may have to create a solid sub-base with sand and hardcore, consisting of broken bricks, stones, and rubble. This must be well compacted, then covered with a DPC, and the concrete poured.

The depth of a slab will also relate to the size and weight of the structure it will have to support. While a depth of 4 inches is adequate for a pergola or other light structure, you will need to throw a deeper strip foundation around the perimeter of a slab for a building.

A combination square is useful for marking cutting edges.

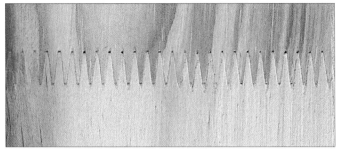

A nail-gun is used by the professionals.

Finger joints are glued at the sawmill (see page 29.)

CARPENTRY

Cutting lumber and joining it to form various garden structures is a reasonably basic skill. Nevertheless, it is very important to ensure that the materials you are working with have the correct dimensions. Measure the wood two or three times, cut it once.

It also pays to be meticulous when working out your requirements. If you buy the wrong lumber, you could end up having to redesign whatever you are planning to build, or even worse, find that it collapses during the first strong wind! It is usually advisable to buy lumber that is a little longer than needed and cut it to size, rather than end up with pieces that are too short.

If you are uncertain about the optimum spacing of poles, posts, and other timbers for your particular structure, local manufacturers or suppliers may be able to advise. Otherwise, seek professional assistance before you tackle your project (see pages 9, 11 and 12.)

Cutting wood

Although you will find it easier to make a perfectly square, straight cut if you clamp the wood to a workbench, this is obviously not possible when you are sawing lumber that has already been erected. You may have to ask someone to support the other end of the wood. Start the cut in the correct place and then continue sawing in the same line. If you are working with a handsaw, make a small nick in the edge of the wood by drawing the saw toward you. The angle used to work different saws varies slightly (a flatter position is used with a cabinet saw), but the movement is much the same. Whether you are using a handsaw or power tool, do not force the blade through the wood. Let the blade or the machine do the work.

Working with electric saws takes practice and confidence. Remember that the narrow blade of a jigsaw cuts on the up-stroke, so to minimize splintering, place boards and planks right-side down on the workbench.

Drilling

Wood is reasonably soft and easy to drill. The secret is to make the hole in the right place, and to prevent the bit from splintering the wood.

There are various drill-bits available, but you will generally use either twist-bits or wood-bits. For screws with countersunk heads, you will need a countersink, and to make larger holes, a flat bit. Whichever drill-bit you use, it must be the right size in relation to the nail, screw, or bolt you are using. It is important that pre-drilled holes are the correct depth and that they align with one another. For screws, you will usually have to drill a pilot hole (which is shorter and narrower than the screw) in one piece of wood and a wider clearance hole in the other for the shank. If you are drilling pilot holes for nails, these should also be smaller than the nail itself.

Joining and fixing

Although some gazebo designs might require relatively complex joints and some intricate fretwork, most garden structures rely on quite simple joints. Many are nailed together with only simple butt joints.

Where the wood overlaps another piece, a T- or cross-butt joint may sometimes be used, but halving joints are generally more effective. A half-lap joint, where the ends of two lengths of lumber are notched so that the pieces slot together, is used either to lengthen two shorter pieces or, if they are joined at right angles, to create a clean corner. A cross-halving joint is ideal for railings round the sides of a deck and for some pergola beams. Miter joints are used where the ends of lumber are cut at a 45° angle, resulting in a 90° joint where the pieces abut neatly to form a corner. (See also page 51.) While the basic techniques used when

Working with saws, nails, power tools, chemically-treated wood, and with heavy lumber can be potentially dangerous, so it pays to be sensible and to take precautions. If you stay alert and pay attention to what you are doing at all times, you can avert needless accidents.

Clothing

Although there is usually no need for amateur builders to don hard hats, boots, and gloves, it is important to dress sensibly. Avoid loose clothing or jewelry that could become caught in the moving parts of power tools or machinery, tie back long hair, and wear gloves, boots, and so on when necessary. Safety goggles may seem unnecessary, but they are invaluable in certain circumstances. A face mask is also a good idea where the job involves dust and grit, especially if you are sawing or planing wood that has been pressure-treated with toxic chemicals.

Treated lumber

While structural lumber should be treated with preservatives, there are certain precautions that should be taken when working with it.
• Wear a face mask (see above), especially if you are working in a confined space, as frequent or prolonged inhalation of the sawdust from treated wood can be harmful.

• If possible, work outdoors so that airborne sawdust can disperse.
• Always wash up thoroughly after working with treated lumber.
• Sawdust inevitably settles on clothing, so wash it separately.
• Never burn treated lumber in an open fire, an indoor fireplace, or on a barbecue. The toxic fumes may be dangerous if inhaled and the chemicals can affect food.

Preservatives

When applying preservatives to untreated lumber, extreme caution is necessary. Toxicity varies but most preservatives are poisonous to humans, animals, and plants, at least until they are thoroughly dry. Some are highly flammable, so do not smoke while working with these chemicals.

Tools and equipment

Always choose the correct tool for the job. If you do not have the right equipment, hire it. Always keep the work area properly illuminated, and clean up after every job. Cluttered spaces and untidy workbenches invite injury.

Power tools

Before using a power tool, check that its voltage requirements are compatible with your power supply. A power source with voltage greater than that specified for the tool can result in serious injury. Also keep

children away from these tools and store them so that little hands are not tempted to use them.

Power tools must be well maintained. Keep them clean and check the cords regularly for damage. It is especially important to keep handles dry and free from grease, and to avoid using these tools in a damp environment, or near flammable gases and liquids. If you do not have a helper, use a clamp or vise to hold the lumber while working. Always unplug tools from the power supply when not in use. Remove adjusting keys from tools before switching on.

Construction and maintenance

All structures must be safe. Make certain that all exposed wood is smooth and that, wherever possible, edges and corners are rounded. This is particularly important where a structure is intended for children. Check the structure regularly to ensure that it is sound, and make sure screws and nails do not protrude. Any rusty fasteners should be removed and replaced if they are in any way hazardous. If repairs are necessary, make them straight away, before the structure deteriorates further and becomes dangerous, and repairs become more expensive. Any rotten or badly split wood should be replaced, and surface areas should be regularly oiled, varnished, or painted.

Bridges must be safe, stable, and sturdy. No lumber submerged in a pond must be treated with toxic chemicals.

building wooden structures are discussed on pages 32 to 36, these detailed instructions take them a step further. Basic carpentry skills are illustrated, and two construction methods for garden buildings are shown. These guidelines incorporate two different floor types (a concrete slab which may be screeded and a suspended wooden floor) as well as decking, installation of doors and windows, and erection of a simple roof structure. They also show how to build basic internal walls (or partitioning) and how to insulate walls.

Even though the presentation follows construction of two simple buildings, these instructions are not intended as projects. Instead, they can be adapted and used when tackling the full range of garden structures, from the simplest arbor or pergola to a greenhouse, shed, shack, or cabin.

The post-and-beam design illustrates a building method which is ideal not only for sheds and barns, but also for smaller-scale playhouses and even for animal shelters. The roof structure can be adapted for a pergola with a pitched roof, and the deck built as a freestanding feature.

The stud structure, built with pre-assembled panels, illustrates a method commonly used for garden buildings of all sizes. This is also an approach often suggested for home improvement projects. Since the method is easily adapted, assembly of a typical panel is also explained.

CONCRETE SLAB

Whether you are casting concrete for foundation footings to support a simple lumber structure, or for a solid slab which will form the floor of a garden building to be built from wood, the principles are exactly the same. Of course, if the slab is to act as a foundation, it must be designed and constructed to carry the load of the lumber (and any other materials) used. Also, the method of construction will affect the size and type of all foundations and footings (see pages 34 to 35).

This slab supports a stud structure (see pages 47 to 50), and the 3 inches thick slab is laid on well-compacted fill. Low-strength concrete (cement, sand and stone mixed in the ratio 1:4:4), suitable for most garden buildings, is used.

1 Build the foundation walls on concrete and allow the mortar to set. Fill with hardcore and sand, moisten, and compact well with a punner, leaving about 3 inches of blockwork above the fill.

2 Spread polyethylene over the hardcore, overlapping all joins by 4 inches. This damp-proof membrane forms a moisture barrier and is an essential measure to take against rising damp.

3 Working in batches, mix sufficient cement with sand and 3/4-inch stone in the ratio 1:4:4 and enough water to make it workable. Pour the mixture over plastic to top of blockwork to form the slab.

4 Use a straight-edged length of wood, such as a 2x4, to compact and level the concrete with the top of the foundation walls. If the slab is not square and level, the wall panels will not fit.

5 While you are laying the slab, bend and insert galvanized hoop iron strapping or steel strips in the concrete (or hollow blocks) at regular intervals around the perimeter, to coincide with the studs.

Post-and-beam building is one of the oldest and most basic systems of construction. The method demands minimal preparation of the site, even on sloping ground, and structures are quick and easy to erect. Although basic carpentry skills (including experience with power tools and a knowledge of fixing and fastening techniques) will be a help, even an unskilled person can tackle a simple post-and-beam structure successfully.

The versatility of this building method creates many design possibilities, and it may be used for a structure of any size. The one illustrated here is only 25 sq. feet in area, and has a covered deck 40 inches wide. It is about 80 inches high, which is quite adequate for a potting shed, tool shed, or playhouse. A layout of the basic design (page 40) and a drawing of the stud framework (page 42) are included for convenience. The plan is on pages 52 to 53, and includes a materials list, or you may prefer to separate the various elements and design your own garden structure.

MATERIALS
Poles or sawn and planed posts may be used as vertical supports. These are embedded in the ground and attached to horizontal beams which form a framework for the wall siding (see pages 18-19,)

In order to accommodate doors and windows, a stud framework must be built to brace the walls. Factory-assembled frames are easily installed, but the small dimensions of some structures, such as the one shown here, may demand that a smaller-than-usual door is used. The simplest solution is to construct a frame on site using wooden laths.

If relatively weak softwood decking slats are used, these should be quite thick (in this case 4½ x 1½ inches) If a tougher, more resistant wood is used, or if the bearers are closer together, thinner slats can be used.

Although standard bargeboard and fascias may be used to finish the little building, a less expensive and much prettier option is a plywood trim.

1 Mark the layout of the building on the ground, using pegs and string (see plan on page 40.) This shed measures 100 x 120 inches. Use the 3:4:5 method (see page 34) to ensure that all corners are at right angles and the building is square.

2 If there is a deck, you will need to indicate where this will be located. To do this, string a line 40 inches from the front 100-inch mark, using a builder's square for accuracy. To double-check that the layout is square, measure all the diagonals.

3 Cut as much wood to size as possible before you start work. The four bearers are 120 inches long, and the five joists which support the floor-boards, 100 inches long. You may need to trim the wood, using a tri-square to mark the cutting line.

4 Although you can use a hand-saw, it will be quicker, and the cut will be more accurate, if you use an electric circular saw. As neither the joists nor the bearers will be visible, it will not be necessary to plane the cut ends of the wood.

5 The upright posts will have to be firmly anchored in the ground, preferably in a concrete footing. A good way to prevent any vertical wind lift is to drill a hole and insert a metal rod through the lumber a couple of inches from the base.

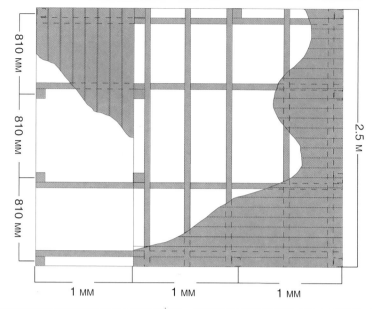

810 MM

810 MM

810 MM

2.5 M

1 MM   1 MM   1 MM

6 The holes for the 14 footings should be at least 20 x 20 x 20 inches in size (see page 35). Dig them all, but only insert the four outside posts, bracing with battens and bricks to ensure that they are vertical.

7 Although many people concrete the posts in at this stage, it is easier to keep the structure square and plumb if you start by securing all bearers, joists, and uprights. Position the two outside bearers first, using blocks of wood to level them.

8 Use the correct drill-bit to bore through the end of each bearer and the base of each of the four upright posts. You will need two coach screws at each point to fasten the lumber. Tighten the screws with a wrench.

9 It is vital that the outside bearers are attached at exactly the same height, or your floor will be uneven. Use a 2x4 with a spirit level placed over it to check. If the ground slopes, one end of the bearers will be off the ground.

10 Now you can position the first joist at the back of the building. Check that it is level and pre-drill holes as before. Use the same length of coach screws to secure the joist to the two posts. Then attach the central and front joists of the structure.

11 The next step is to position the remaining upright posts (see step 12) and two inner bearers. This way, you will not have to brace the posts. Once these are securely fixed, position the last two joists as shown on the plan and skew-nail to the bearers.

12 The two longest upright posts should be positioned opposite one another, to coincide with the apex of the roof. The four shorter posts should be placed at 32-inch centers at the front of the building, to support the railing and balcony roof.

13 Remove the bracing, but before you do any more, double-check the upper plane of the joists and bearers. Do this at several points to check your work is straight and level. It is easier to rectify errors now than later.

14 If you have used sawn (rather than planed) lumber, you may have to use a rasp or file to trim, flatten, or even out sections of some of the pieces. You are unlikely to need a plane unless the wood is badly bowed. There is no need to sand the wood.

15 Now you can concrete the posts in place. Use a 1:4:4 mixture of cement, sand, and stone and place it in the holes with a spade. If all the posts were vertical when they were bolted, the building will be square. Allow the concrete to set overnight.

16 The first decking slat will have to be cut and notched to accommodate the posts. Position it on the bearers, and then draw a line where you are going to cut out. Accuracy is extremely important, so is best to use a combination square.

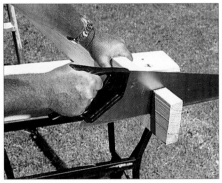

17 The best way to notch lumber is with a handsaw and chisel. This gives better control than a power saw. Work on a stable surface, such as a portable workbench, and use a crosscut saw which is designed to cut across the grain.

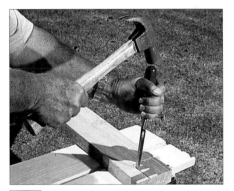

18 Although you can use a saw or a chisel to finish cutting the end joint, you will have to use a chisel to cut the back of the notches which will accommodate the two inner posts. Use a hammer to drive the chisel blade gradually into the wood.

19 String a line along one end of the deck as a guide, then secure the slats with anodized nails. Use a block of wood, planed to the width of the gap you wish to leave between the slats, as a spacer. Trim the other end of the decking as shown in steps 22 and 23.

20 Moving on to the inside of the structure, cut the tongue off the first floorboard and nail the board in place with two oval nails at each of the joists. Continue laying the flooring, slotting the tongue of each board into the groove of each previous one.

21 Line up the ends of all the boards at the front of the building. You will need to notch some of these ends to accommodate the posts, and to trim those which lie at the point where the door is to be hung (see plan on page 42.)

22 Now you can trim the boards at the back of the building. These must line up with the edge of both the bearer and the upright posts. The best way to ensure that the cutting line is straight is to make use of a chalk line, snapping it between two posts.

23 You can use either a handsaw or a power tool to cut the boards. Although you could use a circular saw, it is easier to obtain a really flush cut with a jigsaw. Otherwise use a crosscut saw, following the line marked previously.

24 Before you attach the siding, assemble the roof structure. Use a water level to determine the correct height of all the upright posts. The height of the middle posts will be determined by the required pitch; these are 8 inches higher.

25 Once you have measured and marked all the upright posts, you can cut the excess ends off with a crosscut saw. It is too awkward to use a power saw. Note that the two higher posts should be cut at a slight angle to support the rafters.

26 Before securing the beams, cut a notch at the top of each post, in a dimension which will support the rafters. Then, using coach screws, fasten the beams to the uprights, so that the upper surface of each is flush with the newly cut wood.

27 To prevent the two central beams below the apex of the roof from bowing and bending, sandwich a block of wood between them at the center, and secure with a hexagonal bolt and washer, using a wrench and ratchet to fasten it.

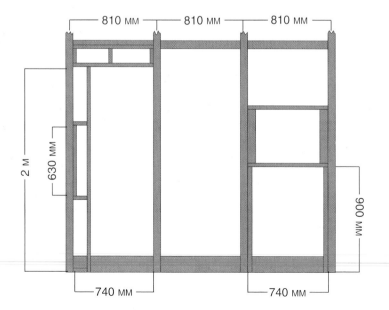

28 You will need eight lengths of lumber for the rafters. Cut them at a slight angle so that they join correctly at the apex. Fix a shorter length to the cut-out posts, and use a combination square to determine the angle.

29 Mark the same angle for all the rafters, checking before cutting the ends. Drill through the rafter and post, then fasten the wood to form a half-lap joint, using a smaller sized coach screw. Repeat at both ends of each rafter.

30 The rafters are joined at the apex with nail-plates, which come in various sizes. Working on the ground, hammer a plate on each side of the wood over the join, or make a plywood gusset.

31 Once all the rafters have been positioned and secured, string a line along the apex of the roof. Use this as a guide when measuring and marking where the purlins should be fixed. Remember to leave a space at the apex for the capping.

32 Now attach the purlins to the rafters with 3-inch long anodized nails. Use the marks made in step 31 as well as the string line to ensure they are nailed on absolutely straight. If the purlins are crooked, the roofing nails will not be neat.

33 Before you lay the roof sheeting, nail the siding to the posts. This splayed lapboard is designed to create a weatherproof wall. Use two nails at each post and check your spirit level periodically to see that the boards are horizontal.

34 While the cladding is nailed across the posts on three walls, the front wall incorporates a door and a window. To brace these openings, it is necessary to build a stud framework (see plan on page 42.) Secure lumber with anodized nails.

35 Studs around the window are nailed to the upright posts, to create an opening exactly the same size as the frame. Although any type of window may be fitted, a PVC frame is one of the easiest to work with, as it simply slots into position.

36 Before the window can be glazed, the frame is screwed to the studs. The inner PVC frame is removed and holes drilled through the frame and into the wood. Countersunk brass screws are used to ensure the frame is flush when it is reassembled.

37 When you reach roof height, it will be necessary to notch the cladding around the purlins and cut it to the angle of the rafters. Use a spirit level as a straightedge to mark the cutting line and then saw the lumber with a crosscut saw.

38 Buy longer lengths of sheeting than required and cut to size. The flexible corrugated sheeting used here is made from organic fiber, which can be cut with an angle grinder or well-oiled handsaw. Mark a line with a chalk line and carefully cut a straight edge.

39 String lines along all edges of the roof to help you keep the roof sheeting straight. Note that the sheeting must overlap at the joins to ensure that it is waterproof. Align the sheets carefully so that the corrugations overlap exactly.

40 Although you usually have to pre-drill holes for roofing nails, you don't need to for organic fiber sheeting so long as you hammer gently. Insert the nails using a spirit level and lines to find the position of the purlins.

41 The ends of the rafters should line up neatly with the ends of the roof sheeting. Use a carpenter's square to mark this point accurately. Then use a crosscut saw to cut all the excess pieces of lumber at the front and back of the shed.

42 The purlins must also be cut so that they are flush with the roof sheeting on both sides. Bargeboard, or in this case a decorative trim, can then be nailed to the ends of the lumber. Once again it is best to use a handsaw to cut the wood.

43 Now attach the capping to close the gap between the sheets which cover the two halves of the shed. Capping must be overlapped like the sheeting. Secure with roofing nails along the purlins.

44 Most of the work has now been done, and now you can make the railing around the deck. First, fix a supporting strut to the shed at the corners of the deck, opposite the two outer posts. Then mark cutting lines on all your crosspieces.

45 As the crosspieces below the rails are angled, the ends of each piece must be cut to form a V at both top and bottom. Use a carpenter's square to draw a straight line down one side of each piece to help you cut in a straight line.

46 Preferably clamp the wood to a portable workbench and use a cabinet saw to angle the corners. It is best to cut all the wood before you start assembling the railing. It is also a good idea to check that you have cut the correct angle.

47 Now cut a housing in the center of each crosspiece so they slot together neatly. It will be slightly angled, depending on the length of the diagonals and where they meet. Mark this position and make a series of cuts halfway through the wood.

48 Chisel out the excess wood from the notch. If the cuts made previously are accurate, you will find that you can simply trim the wood at the baseline. Otherwise you will need to pare away the remainder with the chisel blade.

49 The two diagonals should now slot together neatly. There is no need to fix them at this point, although you can glue them if you wish. Once the crosspieces have been secured to the posts and support struts, the railing will be quite sturdy.

50 You can nail or screw the crosspieces into place, but to avoid splitting the wood, it is best to pre-drill the holes. Use the appropriate drill-bit and angle each hole. The upper sections are affixed to the posts and lower pieces to the decking.

51 If you are using nails, use ones that are anodized and will not rust. Make sure you hammer them in so that the tops are flush with the wood. It is also a good idea to countersink them with a punch and fill the holes with wood filler.

52 Now fit the top railings over the criss-cross by skew-nailing them to the upright posts on each side. A drilled pilot hole will help to prevent the lumber from splitting. Make use of an orbital sander to smooth the edges and round them off neatly.

53 Nail the laths to the inside of the doorway to form a narrow frame along the top and sides, using 2-inch long nails. Then hang the door so that it opens outward, above the upper surface of the deck. Fit the lock and the handles.

54 The quadrant can now be nailed to the four outside corners of the building, using suitable nails. This finishes off the corners neatly. You could also use square lengths of wood or PVC capping similar to that illustrated on page 50.

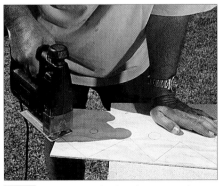

55 Mark the design for your trim on the plywood and cut it out with a jigsaw. Any holes can be made by drilling, using a flat drill-bit. Attach it at the front and sides of the structure with 2-inch nails. Also cut out closures for the capping ends from the plywood.

Stud frame structures are often built with prefabricated panels which are bolted together on site. These are simple to make and no special skills are required.

The method illustrated may be adapted for panels of practically any size, and a range of siding materials may be used. Note that this panel incorporates an optional bracing layer of plywood, which strengthens the structure and improves its insulation qualities.

These guidelines illustrate construction of a typical external panel measuring 120 x 86 inches and in corporating a 46 x 48-inch window. You can make it bigger or smaller, depending on your particular design, although the larger the panel, the more studs you will need to ensure a sturdy framework.

1 The framework of the panel is made with $2^{3}/_{4}$ x $1^{1}/_{4}$ PAR (DAR) lumber. You will need two 120-inch, six 84-inch, three $45^{1}/_{2}$-inch and one $31^{1}/_{2}$-inch lengths, plus two $31^{1}/_{2}$ x 2 x $15^{1}/_{4}$-inch supports for the window.

2 Ensure that all panels are absolutely square. Work on a flat surface and use a carpenter's square to check all corners. If you have a large table, affix short horizontal and vertical battens to guide you.

3 Using 4-inch wire nails, join an 84-inch length of wood to one of the two 120-inch lengths. Note how the smaller battens, secured to the table, help keep the woodwork straight and square. Nail all the pieces together.

4 Make sure the gap you have left for the window is exactly the same size as the frame – in this case, 46 x 48 inches. If it is, you can slot the window-frame into place. Wooden, PVC, and aluminum frames may be used.

5 Nail or screw the window frame securely into place, depending on the type of frame you have used. Note the two 46-inch lengths of wood which must be inserted above the top of the window frame to ensure a snug fit.

6 You will need four pieces of $1^{3}/_{4}$-inch plywood for the bracing layer, 2 x $37^{1}/_{4}$ x $86^{3}/_{4}$-inches, 1 x 46 x $34^{1}/_{2}$-inches and 1 x 46 x $4^{1}/_{2}$-inches for the small section above the window. This should give the structure added strength.

7 Make sure that the plywood is cut accurately and fits neatly over the framework, then use clout nails or round-head nails to secure it firmly to the wood. You can also use heavy-duty staples, inserting them with the aid of a staple gun.

8 Use wire nails to fix the cladding to the plywood, with the first board about 4 inches from the bottom. This lets you overlap the foundation with cladding on site. Also overhang boards by $2^{3}/_{4}$ inches on one side of each corner panel.

Stud-frame buildings may be erected on a concrete slab with a prefabricated board floor, or built with wooden strip flooring. Many prefabricated sheds, as well as smaller structures available in kit form, have wooden flooring. However, concrete is an inexpensive option and is the base illustrated here.

There are several ways to assemble a stud-frame structure, and you must decide whether to use pre-made panels (see page 46) or to build the frame on site and then clad it. The framework must be anchored to the foundation or floor, using strapping or steel strips (as shown here), or by bolting it on with ragbolts. Whichever of these fasteners you use, they should be concreted in when the floor or foundation is laid.

While a post-and-beam building has vertical supports extending to roof height, a stud-frame structure has a conventional roof with trusses. Interior walls are also made from prefabricated panels which, like the outer walls, are insulated before being clad with drywall. Joints are taped, then skimmed with gypsum plaster for a smooth finish.

MATERIALS
All studs and rails are made with planed lumber, the dimensions depending on the size and design of the structure. The panels here were made in the same way as those on page 46. Blankets of fiberglass insulation material are set in all panels after erection and drywall is used to finish internal walls.

If you are building a habitable building, it is wise to insulate the roof and walls. Other cladding materials, roof sheeting and insulation are discussed on pages 18, 19, 22, and 31 respectively.

In addition to the lumber required, you will need cement, sand, and stone for the foundations and the concrete slab, a relatively small number of bricks or blocks for the foundation walls, cement and sand for the mortar and screed, and skimming plaster to skim the walls (see page 30 for quantities). A damp-proof membrane of 250 micron polyethylene must be laid under the slab and you will also need rolls of thicker 375 micron DPC for the base of all wall panels.

Various nails, bolts, and screws are also vital to the project.

1 Before you start erecting the wall panels, prepare the concrete foundation or slab (see page 38.) Nail DPC to base of each panel with clout nails. This should be slightly wider than the lumber used. Position panels on the ground around the slab.

2 Make sure all strapping or steel strips bend toward the center. Starting at one of the corners, raise the first panel to a vertical position and brace with a spare batten. This is a hard work and you will need some assistance.

3 The next panel you erect must be at right angles to the first one. Tack the two sections together with nails, preferably electroplated ones. It also helps to brace the two panels with a horizontal stay across the top corner.

4 It is essential to check periodically that the erected panels are vertical. You can use a spirit level or plumb line to do this (see page 32.) If any of the panels are out of line, you will have to remove the nails and reposition them.

5 To simplify construction, a panel with overhanging boards (see page 46, step 8) is used at each corner. To ensure a neat, secure, and watertight join where the panels meet on a straight wall, sandwich foam between the sections at these points.

6 Continue to erect all the external panels in a systematic manner. As the building takes shape, you will be able to remove the temporary bracing. Note that the bottom edge of cladding is not fixed to the structure at this stage.

7 Continue slotting all the panels in place and nailing adjacent sections together. Do so carefully, ensuring that the cladding strips line up exactly at the corners of the building.

8 If internal panels are to be erected, this will be the next step. These are prefabricated in the same way as the external panels, but without the shiplap cladding. Instead, drywall is later nailed to both sides to create a solid wall surface.

9 The internal panels slot together at right angles, partitioning different sections and adding stability to the structure. You will need about five nails to secure adjacent panels to one another and bolts to anchor them into the concrete.

10 When all the panels are in place, but before you bolt them together permanently, check again that each one is vertical and all are correctly aligned with one another. If necessary, use a large, heavy hammer to knock the studs and rails straight.

11 Now you can nail the hoop-iron strapping or steel strips to the framework (each should be directly in front of a vertical stud.) Pull each piece of metal up straight and, using a sharp punch and a hammer, make a hole to facilitate nailing.

12 Use 3-inch long anodized nails to secure the strapping or steel strips to the studs. It is important to realise that the strapping or strips anchor the building to the foundation. Aligning them accurately with the studs will ensure maximum strength.

13 Before you put the roof on, bolt all the wall panels securely together at the top, center, and bottom of each join. Various fasteners are suitable (see page 31), in particular, coach screws or wood-screws, which are used here.

14 Erecting roof trusses and gable ends takes practice and you will need assistance. Although experienced and agile carpenters may be able to raise the roof sections into position without scaffolding, you will probably find this equipment indispensable.

15 The two gable ends are placed on top of the gable walls and securely braced in position with temporary battens. Then the trusses are positioned and fastened with hoop-iron strapping at the points where they meet the wall panels.

16 Bolt the roof panels at the truss and gable ends, as in step 13. If there is a porch, secure the posts, lean-to rafters, and ceiling panels before installing fascia boards, roof sheeting, flashing, capping, and finally bargeboards at the gable ends.

17 Now you can screed the floor with mortar mixed in a 1:5 cement: sand ratio. You can use the concrete slab as a mixing platform, provided it is clean and you smooth the area out carefully later. First mix the dry materials and then add water.

18 Use a shovel to mix thoroughly until you have a thick paste that will spread easily. If the foundation walls were built with hollow concrete blocks, these must be filled before you start covering the slab. Allow to set before screeding.

19 Make sure the surface of the slab is clean before you start laying the screed. It should also be reasonably rough to achieve good bonding. To improve adhesion further, dampen the floor and roughly brush on a cement-sand slush.

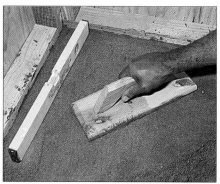

20 It is important to lay the screed before the slush dries. The screed should be about 1 inch thick and well compacted on the slab. Use a wooden float to smooth and level the mortar, checking the accuracy of your work regularly with a spirit level.

21 You can achieve a reasonably flat, uniform surface with a wooden float, or the screed may be lightly smoothed with a steel trowel to get a really even finish. Do not overwork it, or water will rise to the surface and the screed may crack later.

22 If plumbing and electrics are required, get a professional to channel the wiring and pipework in and through the wall before you finish the internal cladding. Then cut the fiberglass insulation to size and pack it into the wall cavities.

23 Working from the floor upward, use galvanized nails to attach the drywall to the studs and horizontal rails at 6-inch centers. Make sure the top of each piece of board is perfectly horizontal and that they join at a stud.

24 Attach drywall to both sides of the internal panels, covering the plywood (on one side) and the framework. This improves the visual finish as well as sound insulation. Trim excess board with a sharp utility knife.

25 One way to install drywall around doors and windows is to cover the opening, mark its position, then cut a hole with a panel saw. If there is more than one sheet of drywall, cut away the first piece then fix the next.

26 Once the board is in place, attach baseboard at floor level. If you wish to plaster around window openings to finish them off neatly, rather than fixing a wooden trim or frame, you can nail or staple on steel or aluminum corner beading.

27 If internal doors do not have their own frames, you will have to use wooden laths to cover the rough edges of the drywall. You can then hang the door, using two hinges and screws. Prop it up while you work so that it clears the floor.

28 Even though the pieces of drywall are abutted against one another, there are invariably slight gaps between them. To disguise these, first fill with a small amount of skimming plaster, then press jointing tape across the filler.

29 The same skimming plaster, which is mixed with water according to the manufacturer's instructions, can then be used to skim over all the joints and nailheads. Alternatively, you can skim the entire wall with gypsum plaster.

30 The front door can now be positioned. It is best to use a door that is supplied with its own frame. This should be nailed or screwed into the opening left in the front wall panel. Use a spirit level to make sure that the door frame is vertical.

31 You will need four hinges to hang a stable door, as well as handles, a lock, and bolts. Since the bottom of the door is difficult to reach once it has been hung, seal this surface before hanging to protect it from excessive weathering.

32 The final steps include installing guttering and downpipes (if required) and fixing the external skirting to overlap the foundation walls. The outside corners of the building can be neatly finished with a PVC cover or with lumber.

JOINTS

Whatever you are going to build, it will be necessary to join separate pieces of lumber together. In most instances, relatively simple joints may be used, but it is always essential to ensure that the connection is strong enough to withstand the strains to which it will be exposed.

BUTT JOINTS

The simplest of all wood connections, butt joints involve abutting wood without making any special cuts in the wood, such as rebates or tongues. Glue, nails, screws and other fastening devices are used to fix the timbers in place.

Butt joints may be used at a corner or where two lengths of lumber meet to form a T. Although a cross-butt joint may be created where two lengths of lumber interconnect, halving joints are usually preferable in this situation.

HALVING (OR HALF-LAP) JOINTS

Simple to perfect, neat halving joints are used for many garden structures including the connection of pergola beams to posts. Cross-halving joints are particularly useful where diagonal timbers cross beneath the railing of a deck.

As their name suggests, halving joints necessitate cutting a rebate equal to half the thickness of the wood, usually from both the timbers to be connected. This results in a strong, interlocking join with a flush surface.

With experience, you will find that measuring tools are not necessary to cut halving joints. Simply mark out the cutting lines with the second piece of lumber, and remember to cut inside the marked line.

HOUSING JOINTS

Similar to halving joints, housing joints involve only one rebate or groove to support the adjoining piece of lumber. These are useful when constructing a stud framework.

MITRED JOINTS

Essentially decorative butt joints, these are found wherever two pieces of wood meet at 45°. Although a standard mitre is not particularly strong, it is a neat joint for many simple garden structures. Alternatively, a mitred halving (or half-lap) joint may be used.

MORTISE-AND-TENON JOINTS

Not common in the average garden structure, mortise-and-tenon joints are sometimes used for pergolas. These involve cutting a rectangular 'mortise' or hole in one

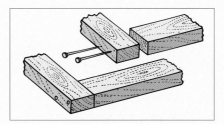

Simple butt joint

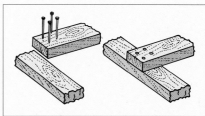

T-butt joint

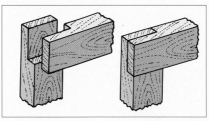

Corner halving joint

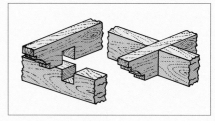

Cross-halving joint

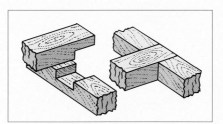

T-halving joint

Mitred halving joint

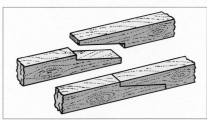

Three-cut scarf joint

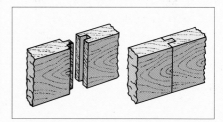

Tongue-and-groove joint

piece of lumber, and a 'tenon' or tongue to fit into the second. The two lengths of wood then slot together. Although the standard mortise-and-tenon joint is neat, it is not always strong enough.

POLE JOINTS

Even though most structures built with poles do not require elaborate joints, it is useful to know how to adapt methods to fit their cylindrical form. In some instances, poles may be abutted to one another, but simple halving joints are usually a more adequate option, and housing joints are particularly useful where horizontal and vertical timbers need to be connected.

SCARF JOINTS

Used to lengthen timbers, rails, beams and so on, scarf joints are usually glued, clamped and pinned. The simplest kind is made by cutting the ends of both pieces of wood at an angle and attaching them in a straight line This type of joint will be considerably stronger if made with three saw cuts, but they must be accurately marked.

TONGUE-AND-GROOVE JOINTS

Particularly common for floorboards and cladding, tongue-and-groove joints are often found where manufactured lumber boards have been used. The tongue fits into the groove, creating a nice, snug finish.

DESIGNS AND PLANS

This charming garden shed may be used as a storeroom for tools and garden equipment, or even as a workroom or children's playhouse. Designed with a narrow deck in front, the building is constructed by assembling a post-and-beam frame on site. The roof is covered with organic-fiber sheeting, a flexible, corrugated roof covering which is lightweight and easy to install. It could be insulated and clad with drywall inside. Simple wooden cut-outs and a criss-cross railing add charm and character, while paint gives it a traditional look.

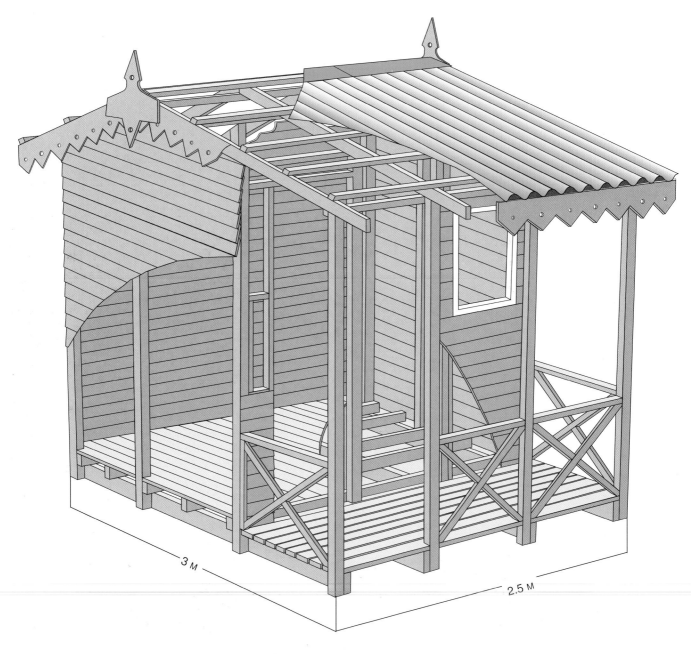

3 M

2.5 M

MATERIALS

Footings
880 pounds cement
48 cu. inches sand
48 cu. inches stone

Lumber
4 x 100 x 9^1/$_4$ x 2 inch bearers
5 x 110 x 6 x 2 inch joists
14 x 128 x 2^3/$_4$ x 2^3/$_4$ inch
  upright posts
8 x 110 x 4^1/$_4$ x 4^1/$_2$ inch
  decking slats
25 x 80 x 4 x 8^1/$_2$ inch tongue-
  and-groove floorboards
1 x 80 x 2^3/$_4$ x 8^1/$_2$ inch stud
2 x 3 x 2^3/$_4$ x 8^1/$_2$ inch studs
1 x 25^1/$_4$ x 2^3/$_4$ x 8^1/$_2$ inch stud
3 x 11^1/$_4$ x 2^3/$_4$ x 8^1/$_2$ inch
studs
3 x 4^1/$_4$ x 2^3/$_4$ x 8^1/$_2$ inch studs
2 x 36 x 2^3/$_4$ x 1^1/$_2$ inch studs
1 x 3 x 2^3/$_4$ x 1^1/$_2$ inch studs
2 x 24 x 2^3/$_4$ x 1^1/$_2$ inch
stud
1 x 24 x 1^1/$_2$ inch x ^{1}/$_4$ inch
  laths
2 x 7^3/$_4$ x 2^1/$_4$ x ^{1}/$_4$ inch laths
5 x 100 x 3 x 1^1/$_2$ inch
  beams
1 x 4 x 2^2/$_4$ x 1^1/$_2$ inch spacer
  block
4 x 82^3/$_4$ x 4^1/$_4$ inch x 1^1/$_2$ inch
  rafters
4 x 42^3/$_4$ x 4^1/$_4$ inch x 1^1/$_2$ inch
  rafters
8 x 104 x 2 x 1^3/$_4$ inch purlins
40 x 120 x 5^1/$_4$ x ^{3}/$_4$ inch
  lapboards
42 x 100 x 2 x ^{3}/$_4$ inch
  lapboards
2 x 28^1/$_2$ inch x 1^1/$_2$ inch x ^{3}/$_4$
  inch rail supports
8 x 48 x 1^1/$_2$ inch x 1^1/$_2$ inch
  crosspieces
2 x 36 x 2^3/$_4$ inch x 1^1/$_2$ inch
  rails
2 x 3 x 2^3/$_4$ inch x 1^1/$_2$ inch
  rails
4 x 108 x ^{1}/$_2$ inch quadrants
140 x 8 x ^{1}/$_2$ inch piece
  plywood

Roof covering
3 x 36 inch wide roof cappings

3 x 40 x 39 inch corrugated
  organic-fiber roof sheeting
3 x 80 x 38^3/$_4$ inch corrugated
  organic-fiber roof sheeting

Doors and windows
24 x 76 inch door
24 x 24 inch PVC window frame
22 x 22 inch safety glass

lock set with handles

Fasteners
14 x 12 inch long reinforcing
  rods
62 x 3^1/$_4$ x 4-inch coach
  screws
16 x 2^1/$_4$ x 2^1/$_2$ inch coach
  screws
1 x 3^1/$_4$ x 6 inch hexagonal
  bolt with washer
4-inch anodized wire nails
3-inch anodized wire nails
2-inch anodized wire nails
oval flooring nails
10 x 2^1/$_2$ inch countersunk
  brass screws
2 x nail plates
  (lumber connectors)
80 x 2^3/$_4$ ring-shank roofing
  nails with cover
2 x hinges with screws

This perfectly proportioned pergola will be a decorative addition to any garden. Designed to provide a sturdy and stable support for climbing plants, it incorporates a series of criss-crossed rails which add a feeling of

1 Insert reinforcing rods into each post, 1 inch from the base.
2 Dig 14 foundation footings, 20 x 20 x 20 inches.
3 Set four corner uprights in holes and brace.
4 Secure two outer bearers with 4-inch coach screws.
5 Secure the central two outer joists with 4-inch coach screws.
6 Position remaining 10 uprights and fasten inner bearers with 4-inch coach screws.
7 Skew-nail last two joists to bearers.
8 Pour concrete into footings and allow to set overnight.
9 Trim tops of uprights to size, as indicated.
10 Fix decking slats to bearers at front of building, using 3-inch nails.
11 Fix floorboards to joists using oval nails.
12 Assemble stud framework to accommodate door and window as shown on page 41. Secure with 3-inch and 2-inch nails.
13 Screw window frame into place.
14 Assemble the roof structure by securing the beams with 4-inch coach screws and the rafters with 5^1/$_2$-inch coach screws, creating a half-lap joint. Join central rafters with nail plate.
15 Affix purlins to rafters with 3-inch nails, leaving space for capping at the apex.
16 Nail the siding on horizontally. Notch around purlins and cut to angle of rafters.
17 Nail roof sheeting to purlins and affix capping at apex.
18 Trim all excess wood from roof structure.
19 Cut decorative trim from plywood and nail across ends of rafters at the front, and purlins at the sides with 2-inch nails.
20 Cut plywood closures for the capping ends and nail in place.
21 Nail rail supports to front wall opposite corner posts and then assemble railings. Notch crosspieces so they fit snugly.
22 Nail quadrant to outside corners with 2-inch nails.
23 Glaze window.
24. Hang door, fit lock set and handles, and finally paint the structure.

This charming shelter can be nailed together in a weekend and erected anywhere in the garden. Upright poles, machined to a reasonably uniform size, combine with sawn and planed lumber to create a rustic venue for seating and alfresco summer meals. Although the surface under the wooden umbrella is grass, it could be paved at a later stage.

MATERIALS

Foundations
230 pounds cement
1023 pounds sand
1023 pounds stone

Framework
4 x 100-inch upright poles, $3^3/_4$ inches in diameter
1 x 20-inch pole for roof, $3^3/_4$ inches in diameter
2 x 140-inch x $2^3/_4$ x $1^3/_4$ 68 inch beams
12 x 68 x $2^1/_2$ x 1 inch roof timbers
8 x $54^1/_2$ x $1^3/_4$ x 1 inch roof timbers

4 x $10^1/_2$ x 1 x 1 inch roof timbers
$3^3/_4$ x $^1/_4$ inch slats to cover 1320 sq. feet
4 x 100 x $2^3/_4$ x 1 inch fascia boards
4 x 68 x $2^3/_4$ x $^1/_4$ inch cover strips
1 x 8 x 8 x $1^3/_4$ inch capping to fit on central apex of roof

Fasteners
4-inch anodized wire nails
2-inch anodized wire nails

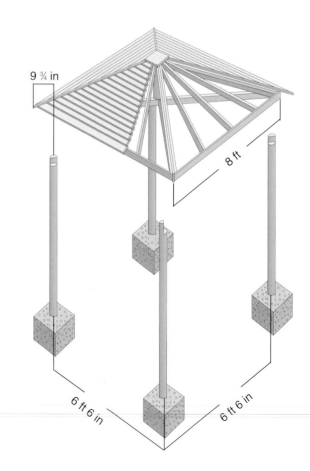

1 Dig four foundation footings, 20 x 20 x 20 inches.
2 Set upright poles in holes, brace, and pour in concrete. Allow to set thoroughly, at least overnight.
3 Assemble basic roof framework by joining two beams at the center with a lap joint and nailing the short pole above the joint. Create the umbrella shape by nailing four 68-inch roof timbers to connect the top of the pole with the four ends of the beams.
4 Working on a flat surface, nail five roof timbers to each side of the roof, as illustrated, to form a support grid for slats.
5 Nail fascia to secure the loose ends of roof timbers.
6 Cut slats to fit and nail over grid, overlapping each one slightly.
7 Nail the cover strip along the upper surface to strengthen and neaten the four corners and affix the capping to the central apex.
8 Cut a $2^3/_4$-inch deep notch in the top of each pole (see detail photograph) and slot the assembled roofing into place. Use 4-inch nails to fasten.
9 Coat with a suitable wood sealer.

9 ¾ in

8 ft

6 ft 6 in

6 ft 6 in

intimacy by partially enclosing the structure. The floor surface features reconstituted flagstones with ground cover planted between them. All the wood has been planed to a smooth finish. The dimensions given relate to the finished size. Upright posts, measuring 5¹/₂ x 5¹/₄ inches, are made from two lengths of 5¹/₂ x 3³/₄ inch lumber, glued together and chamfered for effect.

Numbers in bold refer to illustrations.

1 Dig 12 foundation footings, 20 x 20 inches, to support 96-inch upright posts, and four smaller ones measuring 12 x12 x 12 inches for the short uprights.

2 Bolt the post-anchor bracket or metal shoe to the 96-inch posts and drill a hole in the 30³/₄-inch uprights to accommodate the galvanized pipe.

3 Place anchors (with uprights attached) and pipe in holes and brace.

4 Pour concrete into all footings and allow to set overnight.

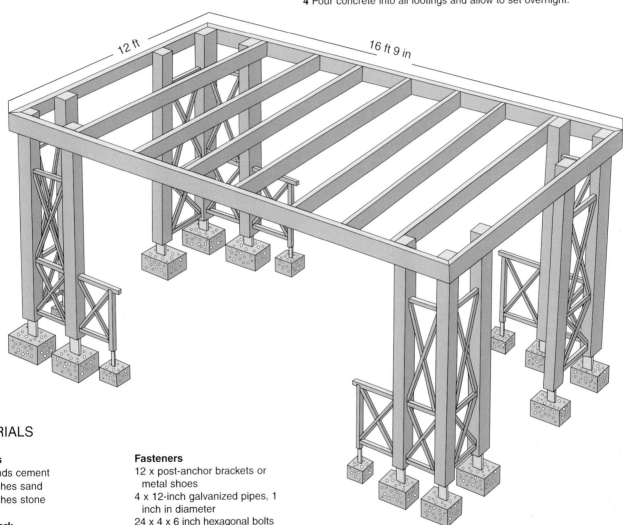

MATERIALS

Footings
814 pounds cement
44 cu inches sand
44 cu inches stone

Framework
12 x 96 x 11³/₄ x 11¹/₂ inches
  upright posts
4 x 30³/₄ x 2³/₄ x 2³/₄ inch upright
  posts
28 x 20 x 3³/₄ x 2¹/₂ inch rails
4 x 22 x 3³/₄ x 2¹/₂ inch rails
16 x 48 x 2¹/₂ x 1¹/₄ inch
  crosspieces
24 x 30¹/₂ x 2³/₄ x 1¹/₄ inch
  crosspieces
2 x 204x 8³/₄ x 1¹/₄ inch beams
9 x 147³/₄ x 8³/₄ x 2¹/₂ inch
  beams

Fasteners
12 x post-anchor brackets or
  metal shoes
4 x 12-inch galvanized pipes, 1
  inch in diameter
24 x 4 x 6 inch hexagonal bolts
  with washers
60 x 3 x 4 inch coach screws
2¹/₂ inch oval, anodized wire nails
4 x 8¹/₄ x 8¹/₄ inch sheets
  galvanized metal
2-inch anodized wire nails
8 x 8¹/₄ x 6¹/₄ inch sheets
  galvanized metal
83 feet 4 inches galvanized wire
  (optional)

5 Slot remaining uprights securely onto protruding pipe.

6 Affix all rails and crosspieces with oval nails as indicated, trimming lumber where necessary.

7 Cut the ends of all four beams to allow for mitered joints at the corners.

8 Position the two longer beams and then, starting at one end, secure shorter beams at equal intervals (approximately 25-inch centers) using coach screws.

9 Bend 4 inches over on each side of the metal to be used for capping. Nail the larger pieces to the tops of the corner uprights, and the smaller ones to the remaining posts.

10 Stretch and secure wire over beams for extra plant support, if desired.

11 Paint, varnish, or seal.

A PLACE TO PLAY

Perfect for adventurous children, this delightful play structure incorporates a hide-out, ladders, and ramps, a deck for outdoor play, and two swings. Essentially a pole structure, the covered hide-out is enclosed with rounded loglap cladding, while both inside and outside decking slats are planed (or dressed) lumber. The ladder into the hide-out is constructed of poles, while the net ladder leading from it is made by knotting synthetic fiber rope to form sturdy webbing between two strong poles. A climbing frame for budding gymnasts has galvanized-pipe rungs. Although the structure photographed is on a slope, to simplify the project, these instructions assume you are building on flat ground. When building on a slope, start from the lowest point and vary the footing depths where necessary.

MATERIALS

Footings
715 pounds cement
40 cu.inches sand
40 cu. inches stone

Pole framework
4 x 144-inch poles, 11 inches in diameter
1 x 120-inch pole,11 inches in diameter
3 x 84-inch poles,11 inches in diameter
2 x 120-inch poles for swing A-frame, $3^3/_4$ inches in diameter
2 x 72-inch pole beams, $3^3/_4$ inches in diameter
2 x $45^3/_4$-inch pole beams, $3^3/_4$ in diameter

Decking and cladding
4 x 44 x $4^1/_4$x$1^1/_4$ inch decking slats
3 x 40 x $4^1/_4$ inch x $1^1/_4$ inch decking slats
2 x 35 x $4^1/_4$ inch x $^1/_4$inch decking slats
14 x 36 x $4^1/_4$ inch x $1^1/_4$ inch decking slats
1 x 72 x 3 inch rail
1 x 36-inch split-pole rail, 36 inches in diameter
4 x $28^1/_2$ x 2 x $1^1/_4$ inch battens
16 x 56 x 4 x $^3/_4$ inch lengths loglap cladding

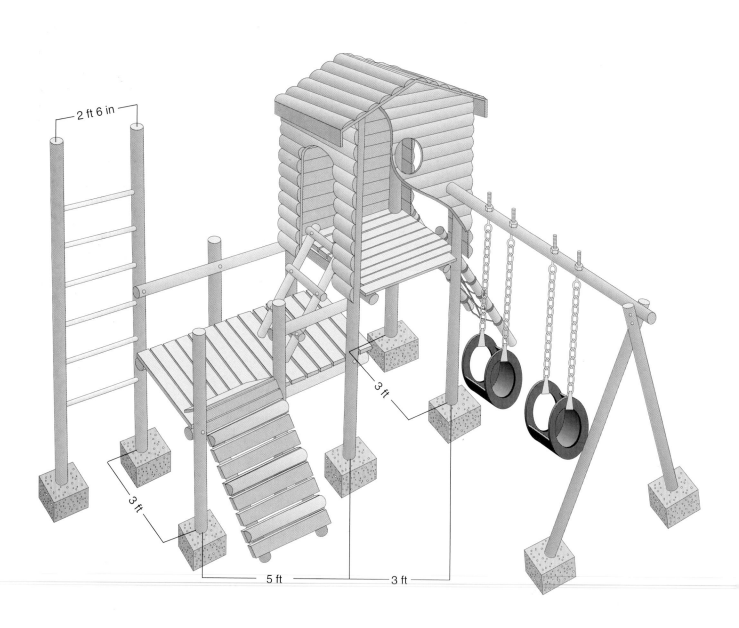

2 ft 6 in

3 ft

3 ft

5 ft

3 ft

38 x 45½ x 4 x ¾ inch lengths loglap cladding
38 x 12¼ x 4 x ¾ inch lengths loglap cladding
2 x 40 x 4 x ¾ inch lengths loglap cladding
4 x 56¼ x 1 x ¾ inch lumber corner pieces
4 x 36 x 1 x ½ inch cover strips

Ladders
2 x 120-inch poles,11 inches in diameter
6 x 32-inch galvanized pipes, 1¼ inches in outside diameter
2 x 60-inch poles, 3¾ inches in diameter
2 x 56-inch poles, 3¾ inches in diameter
2 x 32-inch poles, 2¾ inches in diameter
3 x 22-inch poles, 2¾ inches in diameter
9 x 36 x 4 x ¾ inch slats (treads)
2 x 27¼ x 4 x ¾ inch slats

(treads)
3 x 36-inch split poles, 3¾ inches in diameter
Synthetic rope for webbing

Swings
4 x 52-inch lengths galvanized chain with ¹⁄₁₆ inch link
4 x swing fittings (including bolts etc.)
2 x bucket tyre seats***

Fasteners
1 x 4¾ inch x 9 inch coach bolt
12 x 4¾ inch x 8 inch coach bolts
5-inch anodized wire nails
4-inch anodized wire nails
3-inch anodized wire nails
2-inch clout nails
2-inch anodized wire nails
2-inch oval nails
2 x small nail plates (lumber connectors)

5 Pour concrete into the footings and allow to set overnight.
6 Bolt pole beams to uprights to form firm, level support for decking.
7 Affix 36-inch long decking with clout nails to form lower deck.
8 Nail rest of decking to upper-level beams with 40-inch slats in the center to accommodate pole ladder, and insert short slats between the corner poles.
9 Now assemble simple roof structure of hide-out using 28½-inch battens, mitered and joined with connectors at the center. Height at the apex should be about 58 inches from the floor of the enclosed area.
10 Using oval nails, attach cladding to all four sides of hide-out, placing shorter pieces to create two entrances. Using a jigsaw, cut archways at the top of each entrance to the hide-out.
11 Continue to nail cladding over battens to form roof; use two 45½-inch lengths on two sides as fascias.
12 Cut two 40-inch furring strips to shape to fill triangular spaces between the roof and the walls; if necessary trim the wood below to fit roof shape.
13 Nail the cover strip on the sides of entrances to finish.
14 Use a jigsaw to cut a circle and a triangle for windows in the other two walls.
15 Cut a 10½ inch hole in one wall to allow the 120-inch horizontal pole of the swing frame to enter the enclosure. Secure to upright pole with a 9¼-inch coach bolt and to A-frame with smaller bolt.
16 Nail safety rails to lower deck structure, leaving space alongside split-pole rail for ramp entry.
17 Make the pole ladder by nailing 2¾-inch thick poles, together with 11-inch wire nails. Cut one end of longer poles at a slight angle and skew-nail firmly to deck and upper platform.
18 Construct ramp using 60-inch poles as stringers (on sides). Nail two 34-inch treads at top to accommodate poles supporting deck.
19 Nail split poles on 2nd, 5th, and 8th tread for extra foothold.
20 Cut out the last slat to accommodate the stringer poles and attach at 45° to the platform.
21 Position poles for net ladder 32 inches apart and skew-nail to structure. Knot rope to form webbing.
22 Affix swing chains and tire seats securely to horizontal pole.
23 Sand, and oil, or seal.

1 Mark the layout of the structure and then dig all 11 footings to at least 20 x 20 x 20 inches.
2 Assemble pipe ladder using two 120-inch long poles, inserting metal rungs into holes drilled out at 12-inch centers.
3 Place ladder and rest of upright poles into footings and brace. Ensure that the end supports for swings meet to form the A-frame.
4 Secure the A-frame with 8-inch coach bolts.

A charming wooden entrance creates instant appeal and ambience, with the craftsman's attention to detail giving the structure an old-fashioned look. The basic structure is made from decorative lumber posts and neat latticework, while corrugated organic fiber, a flexible sheeting, is used as the roof covering, providing shelter at the front door during bad weather. The design is essentially quite simple, the only complicated carpentry being the turned finial.

MATERIALS

Footings
132 pounds cement
517 pounds sand
517 pounds stone

Lumber
2 x 95 x 3 x 36$\frac{1}{2}$ inch upright posts
2 x 88 x 36$\frac{1}{2}$ x 1$\frac{3}{4}$ inch upright posts

4 x 72 x 3$\frac{3}{4}$ x 1$\frac{1}{4}$ inch rafters
1 x 88 x 4$\frac{1}{4}$ x 1$\frac{1}{4}$ inch beam
1 x 88 x 3$\frac{3}{4}$ x 1$\frac{1}{4}$ inch beam
2 x 38$\frac{1}{4}$ x 3$\frac{3}{4}$ x 1$\frac{1}{4}$ inch beams
6 x 27$\frac{3}{4}$ x 3$\frac{3}{4}$ x $\frac{1}{4}$ inch rails
1 x 1$\frac{1}{4}$ x 3$\frac{3}{4}$ x 1$\frac{1}{2}$ inch brace
6 x 38$\frac{1}{4}$ x 1$\frac{3}{4}$ x 1$\frac{1}{2}$ inch purlins
1 x 39 x 3$\frac{3}{4}$ x 1$\frac{1}{2}$ inch strut
1 x 31$\frac{1}{2}$ x 3$\frac{3}{4}$ x 1$\frac{1}{2}$ inch ridge beam
2 x 21$\frac{1}{2}$ x 3$\frac{1}{4}$ x 1$\frac{1}{2}$ inch corner pieces, cut to shape from 4 x 1$\frac{1}{2}$ inch lumber
4 x 2 inch lapboard, to cover 88 sq. inches
2 x 38$\frac{1}{2}$ x 5$\frac{3}{4}$ x 1$\frac{3}{4}$ inch fascias
2 x 72 x 5$\frac{3}{4}$ x 1 inch bargeboards
2 x 72 x 3$\frac{3}{4}$ x 1 inch cover strips
26 x 40 x 1$\frac{1}{2}$ x $\frac{1}{4}$ inch laths
26 x 37$\frac{1}{2}$ x 1$\frac{1}{2}$ x $\frac{1}{4}$ inch laths
70 x 27$\frac{3}{4}$ x 1$\frac{1}{2}$ x $\frac{1}{4}$ inch laths
8 x 8 x 2 inch x $\frac{3}{4}$ inch lumbers, mitered at each end
16 x 7 x 1$\frac{1}{2}$ x 1$\frac{1}{2}$ inch curved moldings, mitered at each end
1 x 12 inch turned finial

Roof covering
2 x 68 x 38$\frac{1}{4}$ inch sheets corrugated organic-fiber roof sheeting
38$\frac{1}{4}$ inch roof capping

Fasteners
10 x $\frac{1}{4}$ inch x 3-inch anchor bolts
2 x $\frac{1}{8}$ inch galvanized anchor plates
4 x $\frac{1}{4}$ inch x 3-inch coach screws

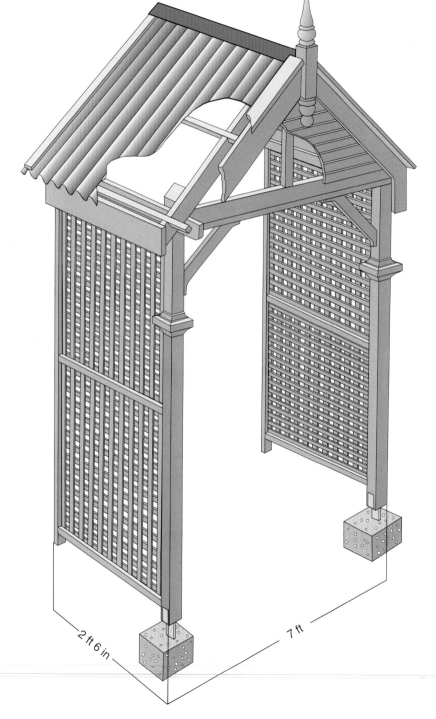

2 ft 6 in

7 ft

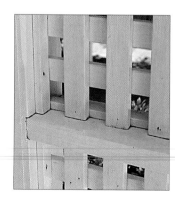

various brass screws (preferably countersunk)
panel pins

24 x 3³/4 inch ring-shank roofing nails with covers
2 x 64 inch flashing

1 Cut and bolt 88-inch upright posts to wall about 80 inches apart, ensuring doorway is centered.

2 Cut 1¹/4 inch x 1³/4 inch notches in 4 rafters to accommodate purlins on edge. Bolt two rafters against wall to form apex of roof.

3 Measure 33 inches from wall and dig two holes. Concrete anchor plates into these and allow to set.

4 Assemble upright front section of framework on the ground using brass screws. Notch the broader 88-inch beam to accommodate upright posts and set the 3³/4-inch beam on edge above it.

5 Lift front section into position, brace temporarily, and fasten to anchor plate using coach screws. Ensure height aligns with framework on wall.

6 Cut notches in upright posts to accommodate 38¹/4-inch long beams, and notches 5³/4 inches from one end of each beam for the rafters. Lay these beams on edge under the eaves (there will be a 5-inch overhang in front).

7 Affix the 27³/4-inch long rails between the posts, with the top one flat against the underside of the top beam. Allow a gap of 37¹/2 inches and 40 inches to the center and bottom beams respectively.

8 Now assemble remaining rafters, bracing at the apex.

9 Cut ends of lumber at the required angles to fit.

10 Screw rafter to upright posts, slot purlins into position and secure.

11 Screw perpendicular strut at front of the structure, behind the rafters and beam.

12 Secure ridge beam in position.

13 Screw corner pieces in place.

14 Now affix the lapboard, working from the bottom up.

15 Nail roof sheeting to purlins and affix capping at apex.

16 Screw fascias to bottom ends of rafters and bargeboard to front of structure. Glue and screw a decorative shaped end (cut from offcuts) to bargeboard if desired.

17 Neaten top of bargeboard with cover strip.

18 Attach laths vertically on sides of structure.

19 Reserve eight 27³/4-inch laths. Make up four lattice panels (two 40 inch x 27³/4inch, two 37¹/4-inch x 27³/4 inches) with a grid of 1¹/2 x 1¹/2 inch, using panel pins to join horizontal and vertical laths.

20 Slot the panels into place and then secure by attaching the remaining laths to the rails.

21 Screw mitered lumber around front posts as shown, finishing off with decorative molding above and below each piece.

22 Screw decorative finial to apex of roof.

23 Fill any screw holes and paint as desired.

24 Attach flashing between the entrance roof and the wall of house.

Even if you do not have any suitable trees, with a little imagination you can erect this tree-house in any garden. The little building, which incorporates a 3-inch wide balcony, is set on two dead, but sturdy, tree trunks which have been concreted into the ground so that they emerge from the tree-house in a natural way. Much of the house is made from exterior-grade plywood, while the flooring is a tongue-and-groove flooring known as shutterboard. Plywood for siding was ripped to 6 inch widths from standard sheets. Although there is no glazing, open spaces in the wall could be adapted to incorporate window frames. A wooden ladder leads onto a covered deck, while a prefabricated slide suggests an easy escape for little people. If softwood is used for bearers, V-bracing, and joists, use similar dimensions to those in the Garden Shed on page 52.

MATERIALS

Footings
220 pounds cement
30 cu. inches sand
30 cu. inches stone

Lumber
2 x 101 x 4¹/₂ x 3¹/₄ inch hardwood bearers
4 x 4¹/₄ x 4¹/₄ x 1¹/₄ inch lengths hardwood for V-bracing
5 x 112 x 4 x 1³/₄ inch hardwood joists
4 x 80 x 3³/₄ x 3³/₄ inch upright posts
2 x 80 x 2¹/₄ x 2¹/₄ inch upright posts
3 x 34 x 2¹/₄ x 1¹/₄ inch upright posts
1 x 30 x 2¹/₄ x 2 inch upright post
2 x 97¹/₂ x 48¹/₂ x ³/₄ inch pieces shutterboard
1 x 48 x 2³/₄ x 1¹/₄ inch sole plate
2 x 44 x 2³/₄ x 1¹/₄ inch sole plates
2 x 36 x 2³/₄ x 1¹/₄ inch sole plates
4 x 30 x 2³/₄ x 1¹/₄ inch sole plates
1 x 26 x 2³/₄ x 1¹/₄ inch sole plate
5 x 78³/₄ x 2³/₄ x 1¹/₄ inch vertical studs
2 x 40 x 2³/₄ x 1¹/₄ inch vertical studs
1 x 37¹/₂ x 2³/₄ x 1¹/₄ inch vertical stud
2 x 92 x 2³/₄ x 1¹/₄ inch horizontal studs
3 x 6¹/₄ x 2³/₄ x 1¹/₄ inch horizontal studs
2 x 36 x 2³/₄ x 1¹/₄ inch horizontal studs

1 x 97¹/₂ x 2³/₄ x 1¹/₂ inch beam
8 x 66 x 2³/₄ x 1¹/₂ inch rafters
³/₈ inch exterior plywood to cover 15 sq.yards, ripped to 6-inch widths
2 x 97¹/₂ x 66 x ³/₈ inch pieces exterior plywood
2 x 100 x 2¹/₄ x 2 inch rails
1 x 32³/₄ x 2¹/₄ x 2 inch rail
2 x 96 x 2³/₄ x 1³/₄ inch stringers
6 x 24 x 2³/₄ x 1⁵/₈ inch rungs
1 x 39¹/₄ x 26 x ³/₄ inch piece shutterboard
1 x 32 x 26 x ³/₄ inch piece shutterboard
1 x 72 x 1¹/₄ x ¹/₂ inch lath
1 x 25¹/₄ x 2 x ³/₄ inch lath

Fasteners and hardware
16 x 1-inch threaded bolts with washers

5 x ³/₈ x 4¹/₄ inch coach bolts
20 x ¹/₄ x 4 inch coach bolts
1³/₄ inch brass screws
1³/₄ inch anodized clout nails (optional)
1¹/₄ inch anodized clout nails
4 x brass hinges with screws
handle set
1 x brass barrel bolt with screws
bituminous felt (or geofabric) to cover 10 sq. yards
fiberglass slide (optional)

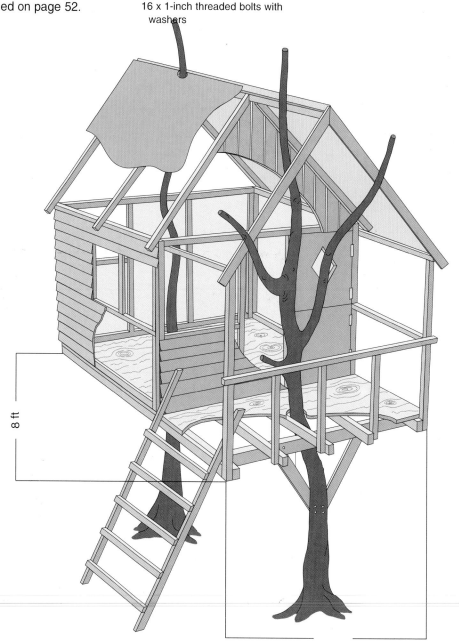

8 ft

7 ft 10 in

1 Dig two 24 x 24 x 24-inch footings in which to "plant" suitable dead trees. First place 8 inches of concrete at bottom of holes, allow to set, then stand trunks on foundations, and fill the holes with more concrete. Allow to set again, overnight. Tops of bearers should be 68 inches from ground level.

2 Erect supportive framework of two bearers and V-bracing (see detail photograph). Use 12 threaded bolts to secure lumber to trees and bearers to bracing.

3 Set joists across bearers, skew-nailing into position.

4 Fix the shutterboard in position with screws to form the floor.

5 Erect four main (3 x 3-inch) upright posts at corners of building, securing to bearers with threaded bolts.

6 Attach 80-inch high balcony posts to the two outside corners with four 4³/₄ inch cuphead bolts.

7 Assemble studs for walls, with sole plates on the floor (see illustration), securing with brass screws.

8 Now position and secure the roof timbers. First anchor a beam to the two trees at the apex using threaded bolts. Attach rafters so that they can be screwed in just above the beam. You can overlap interior rafters, but miter those at the end of the balcony.

9 Use clout nails or screws to affix plywood siding horizontally to outside of stud framework. Start at the bottom and allow each to overlap the next. See illustration for windows and door openings.

10 Use 1¹/₄ inch clout nails to secure plywood roof to rafters, allowing it to overhang walls by about 4 inches.

11 Fill triangular space between cladding and roof with cladding nailed or screwed vertically to top stud and rafter.

12 Secure three 34-inch posts to joists along front of balcony using six of the smaller cuphead bolts.

13 Screw long rail to top of posts. Nail shorter rail along one side, overlapping side of house slightly.

14 Now assemble the ladder, using 14-inch coach bolts to attach the rungs to the stringers.

15 Use a large coach bolt to affix the 30-inch high post at 24-inch center to second balcony post.

16 Using smaller bolts, secure ladder to these two posts.

17 Screw hinges to remaining pieces of shutterboard and then screw to house, with the 39¹/₄ inch length on top.

18 Screw 72-inch lath to opposite side of the opening in place of a door jamb, and shorter lath along inside top of lower section of door.

19 Cut a diamond in the top section of the door (optional) and fit handles and a barrel bolt.

20 A covering of bituminous felt on the roof will repel water. Overlap all edges and affix with clout nails.

21 Position and fix slide if desired.

22 Finally, paint the door, and coat the lumber as desired.

An imaginative addition to any garden, this ornamental aviary incorporates a pitched roof which is constructed in exactly the same way as the Wooden Umbrella on page 54. The rest of the structure consists of four simple panels which incorporate attractive latticework. These, like the roof structure, are pre-assembled and bolted together on site. All four sides are covered with wire mesh, while a door at the back of the aviary makes it easy for a person to enter in order to clean the area and feed the birds.

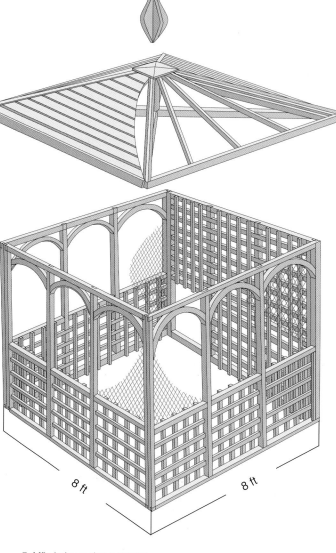

MATERIALS

Framework
12 x 98³/₄ x 1³/₄ x 1³/₄ inch horizontal lumbers, notched to accommodate uprights
16 x 80 x 1³/₄ x 1³/₄ inch upright lumbers, notched to fit into horizontal notching
3 x 30³/₄ x 1³/₄ x 1³/₄ inch arches, cut from 7³/₄ inch wide lumber
6 x 30¹/₄ x 1³/₄ x 1³/₄ inch arches, cut from 7³/₄ inch wide lumber
11 x 98³/₄ x ³/₄ x ³/₄ inch horizontal laths
8 x 95¹/₄ x ³/₄ x ³/₄ inch horizontal laths
4 x 66 x ³/₄ x ³/₄ inch horizontal laths
8 x 80 x ³/₄ x ³/₄ inch vertical laths
4 x 50¹/₂ x ³/₄ x ³/₄ inch vertical laths (above door)
36 x 31¹/₂ x ³/₄ x ³/₄ inch vertical laths
4 x 30¹/₂ x ³/₄ x ³/₄ inch laths
8 x 27³/₄ x ³/₄ x ³/₄ inch laths
2 x 30¹/₂ x 1³/₄ x 1³/₄ inch lumbers
2 x 27³/₄ x 1³/₄ x 1³/₄ inch lumber
1 x 20³/₄ inch pole for roof, 3³/₄ inches in diameter
2 x 140 x 2³/₄ x 1³/₄ inch beams

12 x 68 x 1¹/₄ x 1 inch roof timbers
8 x 54¹/₂ x 1¹/₄ x 1 inch roof lumbers
4 x 50¹/₄ x 1¹/₄ x 1 inch roof lumbers
2³/₄ x ¹/₈ inch slats to cover 272 sq. inches
4 x 100 x 2³/₄ inch x 1 inch fascia boards
4 x 68 x 2³/₄ inch x 1¹/₄ inch cover strips
1 x 8 x 8 x 1³/₄ inch capping
1 x decorative finial (optional)

Fasteners and hardware
1³/₄ inch countersunk brass screws
3-inch countersunk brass screws
1³/₄ inch brass screws
8 x ¹/₄ inch x 3³/₄ inch hexagonal bolts with nuts and washers
4-inch anodized wire nails
2-inch anodized wire nails
netting staples
2 x brass hinges with screws
latch
wire mesh to cover 24 sq. yards

1 Assemble the panels first, by joining lumber together with lap joints, using 1³/₄-inch screws. Affix arches in position on three of the panels using 3-inch screws, positioning shorter lengths at the corners.
2 Lift the first panel into position and brace. Bolt adjacent panels at right angles.
3 Screw four 27³/₄ inch long laths to the inside of the upright posts (under rail) on two side panels.
4 Now attach wire mesh to inside of structure using netting staples to secure. Leave a 27³/₄ x 30¹/₄ high gap for the door.

5 Affix laths to three panels to create latticework between rail and sole plate, with four equally spaced horizontal pieces of lumber on each.
6 Affix laths to remaining panel, leaving gap for door.
7 Use 30¹/₂ and 27³/₄ x 1³/₄ x 1³/₄ inch lumber to make framework of door. Cover with wire mesh and latticework constructed with remaining laths. Hinge to corner post so it opens outwards. Affix latch.
8 Assemble roof structure by following steps 3 to 5 on page 54 (Wooden Umbrella). Affix finial if required.
9 Slot roofing in position and skew-screw at each corner.
10 Follow steps 6 and 7 on page 54 and paint.

Perfect for the traditional English garden, this period-style gazebo incorporates seating on five sides. Not only is it a feature, but it is a pleasant and practical place for alfresco meals. The basic structure of the gazebo is made from planed (or dressed) lumber and the roof is covered with corrugated iron sheeting. A weathervane adds a charming finishing touch. It is a good idea to provide a solid floor underfoot. This one has been paved with clay bricks.

4 ft 6 in

4 ft 6 in

MATERIALS

Footings
385 pounds cement
1540 pounds sand
1540 pounds stone

Framework
6 x 84 x 3³/₄ x 2³/₄ inch upright posts
6 x 92 x 3¹/₁ x ³/₄ inch rafters

6 x 60 x 3³/₄ x ³/₄ inch beams, cut and mitered to fit
1³/₄ x 1³/₄ inch purlins, total length 6 feet, cut to fit roof

Seating and decorative lumber
6 x 66 x 8³/₄ x 3³/₄ inch pieces hardboard, cut to form decorative bargeboard, and trimmed where necessary

5 x 56 x 6¹/₂ x 3³/₄ inch pieces hardboard, cut to form decorative trim
5 x 58 x 2³/₄ x ³/₄ inch beams
5 x 39¹/₂ x 3³/₄ x ³/₄ inch lumber
6 x 17¹/₄ x 2³/₄ x ³/₄ inch lumber
6 x 15¹/₄ x 2³/₄ x ³/₄ inch seat posts
2³/₄ x³/₄ inch slats, total length 100 feet, cut to fit seating
5 x 54 x 5³/₄ x ³/₄ inch rails
5 x 54 x 31¹/₂ x ³/₄ inch rails
10 x 31¹/₂ x ³/₄ inch x ³/₄ inch laths
75 x 44 x ³/₄ inch x ¹/₄ inch laths
12 x 13¹/₂ x 3³/₄ x ³/₄ inch decorative corners, cut to shape

Roof covering
corrugated iron (or other sheeting) to cover 14 sq. yards
150 feet corrugated iron capping

Fasteners and hardware
6 x galvanized post-anchor brackets
12 x 2-inch coach screws

2-inch brass screws
3-inch wire nails
2-inch wire nails
panel pins
66 x galvanized roofing nails (drive screws)
weathervane on cone

1 Dig six holes for footings, 20 x 20 x 20 inches. Concrete post anchors in position and leave to set overnight.
2 Affix posts to anchors with coach screws and brace temporarily.
3 Nail beams to uprights, allowing an overlap of 1³/₄ inches on outside of posts. There should be a 1¹/₄ inch gap at the top of each post to accommodate the rafters.
4 Slot the rafters into place and nail to posts and at the apex, using offcuts of lumber to secure.
5 Cut ends of rafters vertically to overlap the upright posts by 11¹/₄ inches.
6 Now affix purlins at 35¹/₄ inch centers.
7 Nail roof sheeting onto purlins. Nail capping over joins and affix cone of weathervane at the apex.
8 Use 2-inch nails to attach bargeboard to outside ends of rafters.
9 Screw beams between upright posts with the underside at a height of 310 mm above the ground. Trim pieces where necessary.
10 Assemble rest of seat framework, with 17¹/₄-inch lengths resting on beam and seat posts. Screw each join to secure.
11 Screw remaining lumber to outside of seat post, flush with upper surface of framework. Trim wood where necessary.
12 Measure seating area to check for correct slat lengths. Cut and affix five parallel slats on each.
13 Attach back rail by skew-nailing 3¹/₂-inch lumber on edge, between two uprights, with bottom surface 31¹/₂ inches above ground level. Check lengths of wider rails, trimming if necessary, and round two corners with a sander. Affix on top of 3¹/₂-inch rail so rounded edge protrudes outwards.
14 Screw 1¹/₄ x1¹/₄-inch laths to inside of upright posts between back rail and ground.
15 Use panel pins to attach thin laths vertically between rail and posts. Use offcuts for shorter lengths.
16 Place decorative trim over top of latticework under rail, trimming hardwood where necessary.
17 Attach decorative corners at top of upright posts on either side under the eaves, and paint.

INDEX

U.S. CUSTOMARY/METRIC CONVERSION TABLE

To convert the measurements given in this book to metric measurements, simply divide the figure given in the text by the relevant number shown in the table alongside. Bear in mind that conversions will not necessarily work out exactly, and you will need to round the figure up or down slightly. (Do not use a combination of metric and U.S. customary measurements – for accuracy, stick to one or the other system.)

TO CONVERT	DIVIDE BY
inches to millimeters	0.0394
feet to meters	3.28
yards to meters	1.093
sq inches to sq millimeters	0.00155
sq feet to sq meters to	10.76
sq yards to sq meters	1.195
cu feet to cu meters	35.31
cu yards to cu meters	1.308
pounds to grams	0.0022
pounds to kilograms	2.2046
gallons to liters	3.785